PREGNANCY COLORING BOOK

Join our mailing list to be among the first to find out about special offers, discounts and our new releases!

Sign up at:
www.adultcoloringworld.net

Copyright © 2017 Adult Coloring World
All rights reserved.
ISBN-13: 978-1546586258
ISBN-10: 1546586253

@adultcoloringworld

facebook.com/adultcoloringworldbooks

@adultcolorworld

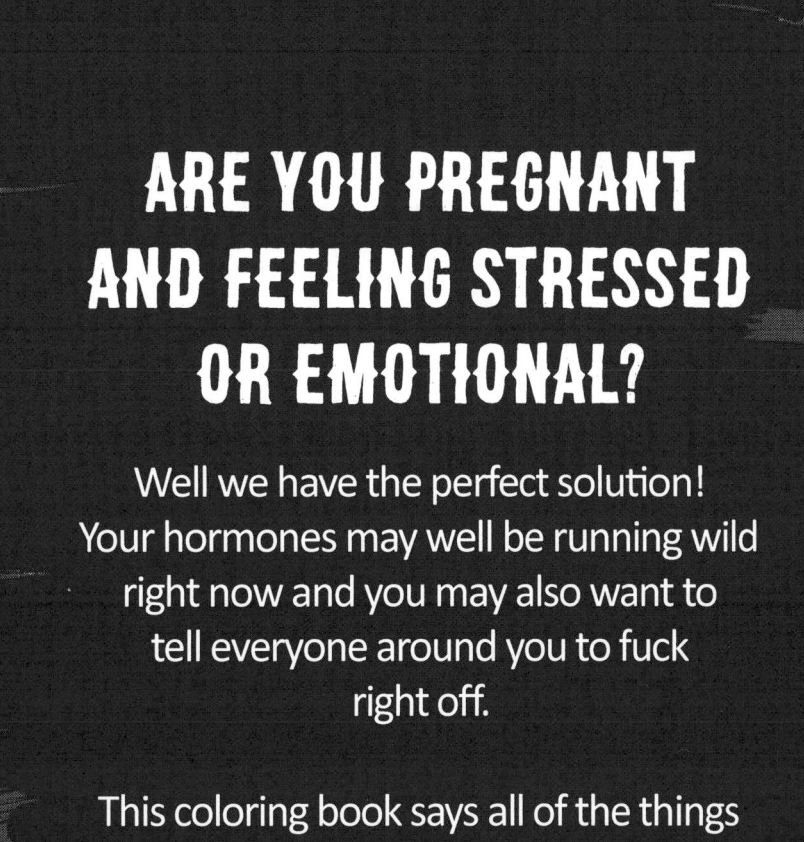

ARE YOU PREGNANT AND FEELING STRESSED OR EMOTIONAL?

Well we have the perfect solution! Your hormones may well be running wild right now and you may also want to tell everyone around you to fuck right off.

This coloring book says all of the things you want to say but can't! So sit back and blow off some steam while coloring these hilarious insults!

ROSES ARE RED

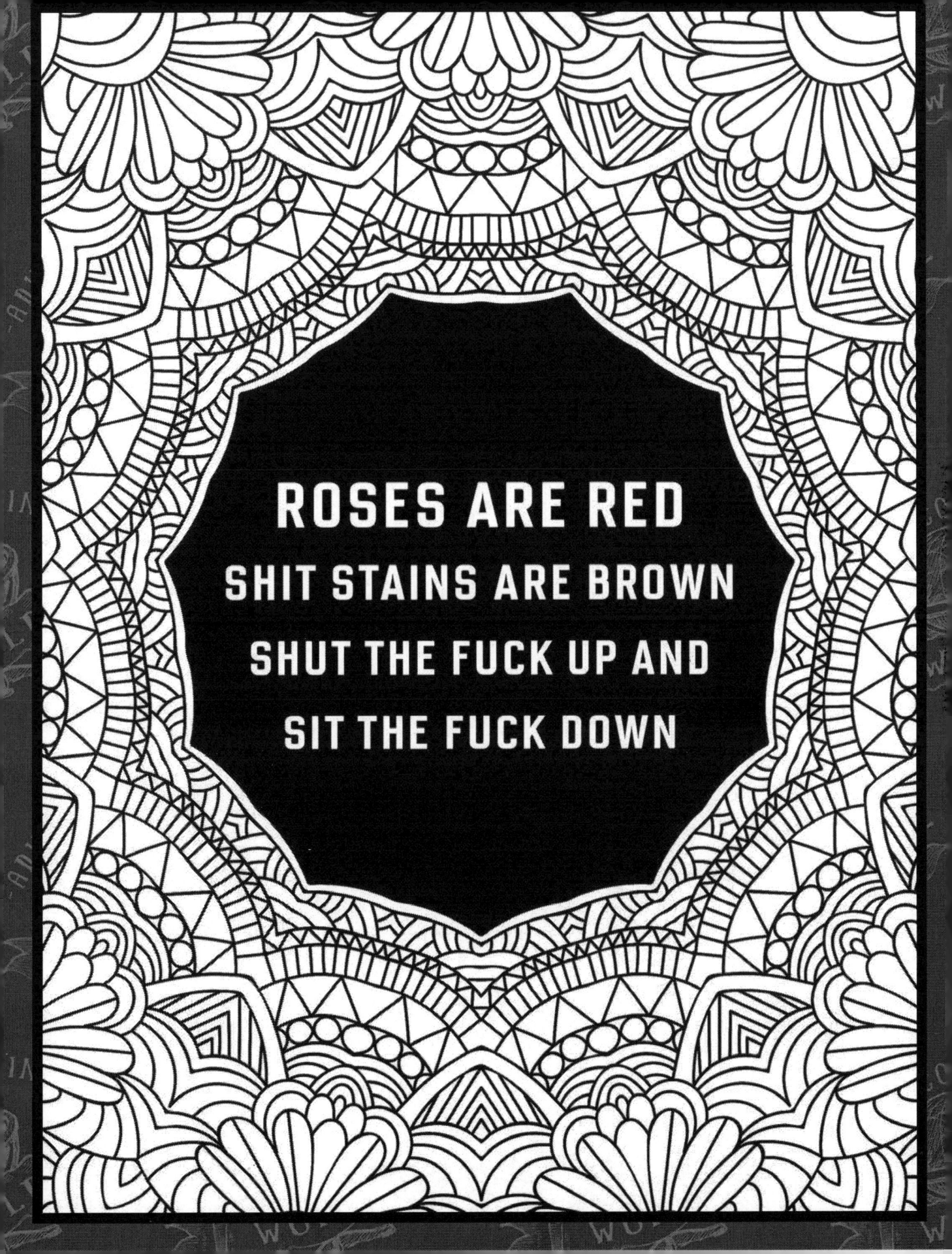

SHIT STAINS ARE BROWN

SHUT THE FUCK UP AND

SIT THE FUCK DOWN

YOUR FACE LOOKS LIKE YOUR FUCKING NECK THREW UP

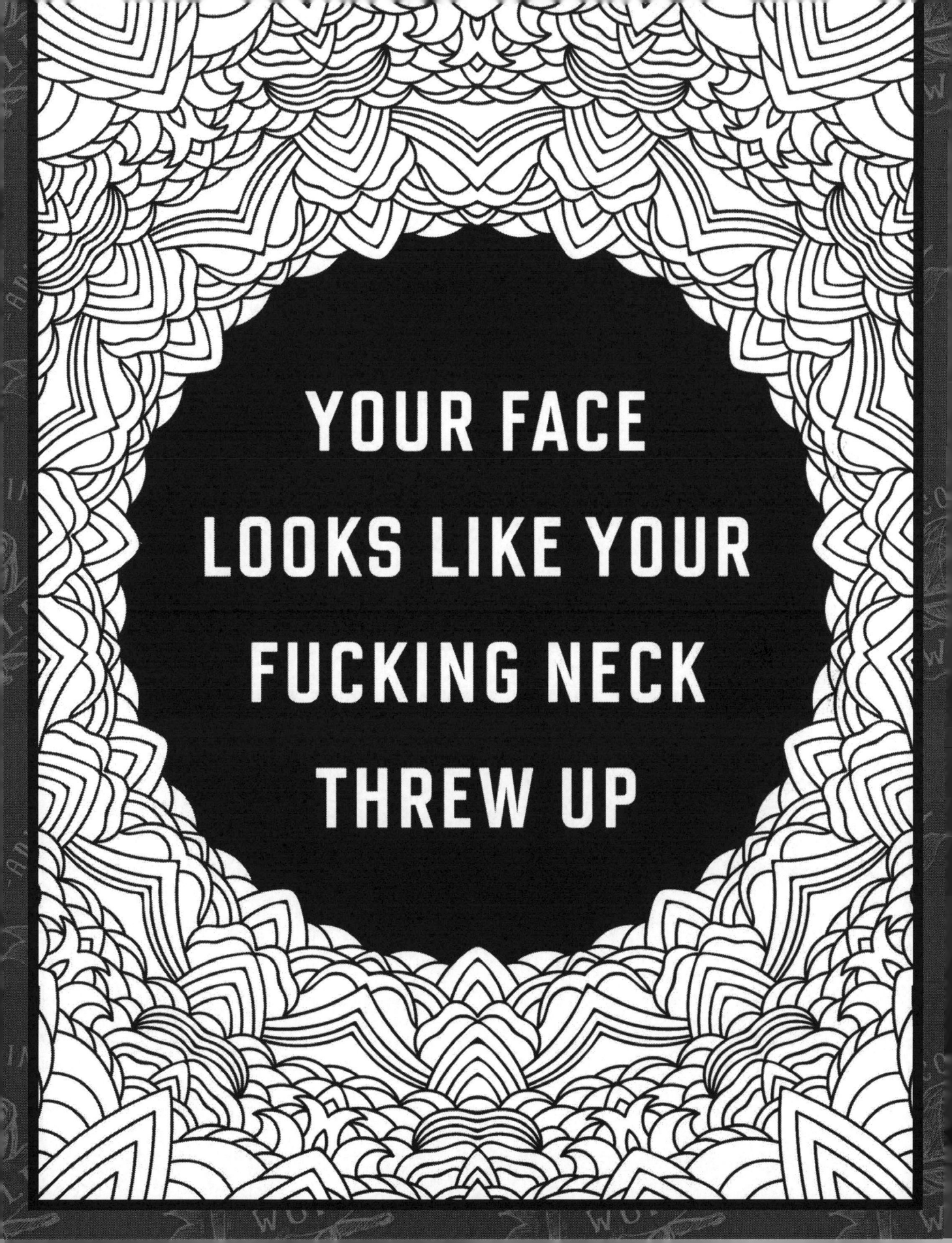

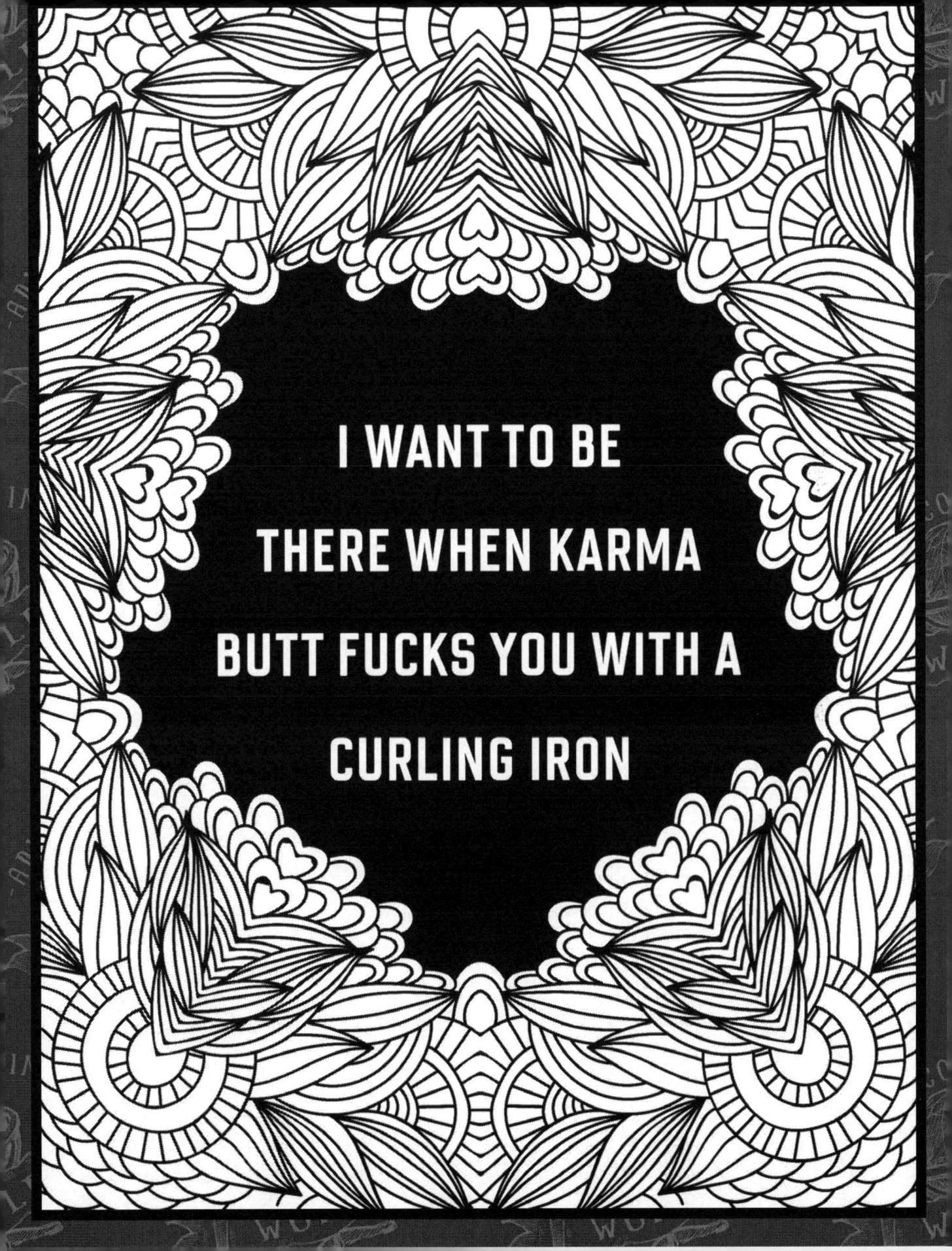

I WANT TO BE THERE WHEN KARMA BUTT FUCKS YOU WITH A CURLING IRON

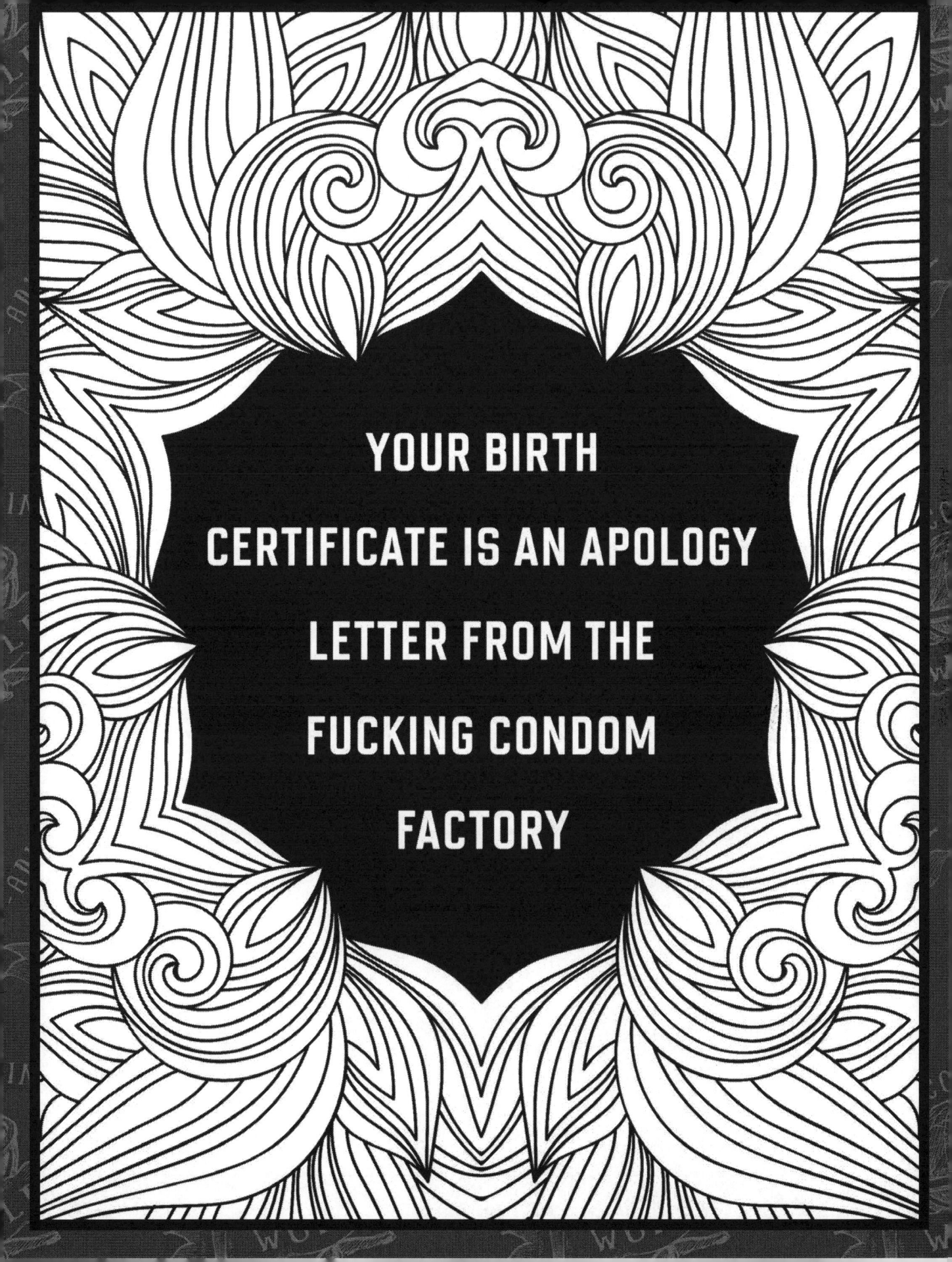

YOUR BIRTH CERTIFICATE IS AN APOLOGY LETTER FROM THE FUCKING CONDOM FACTORY

YOU COULDN'T

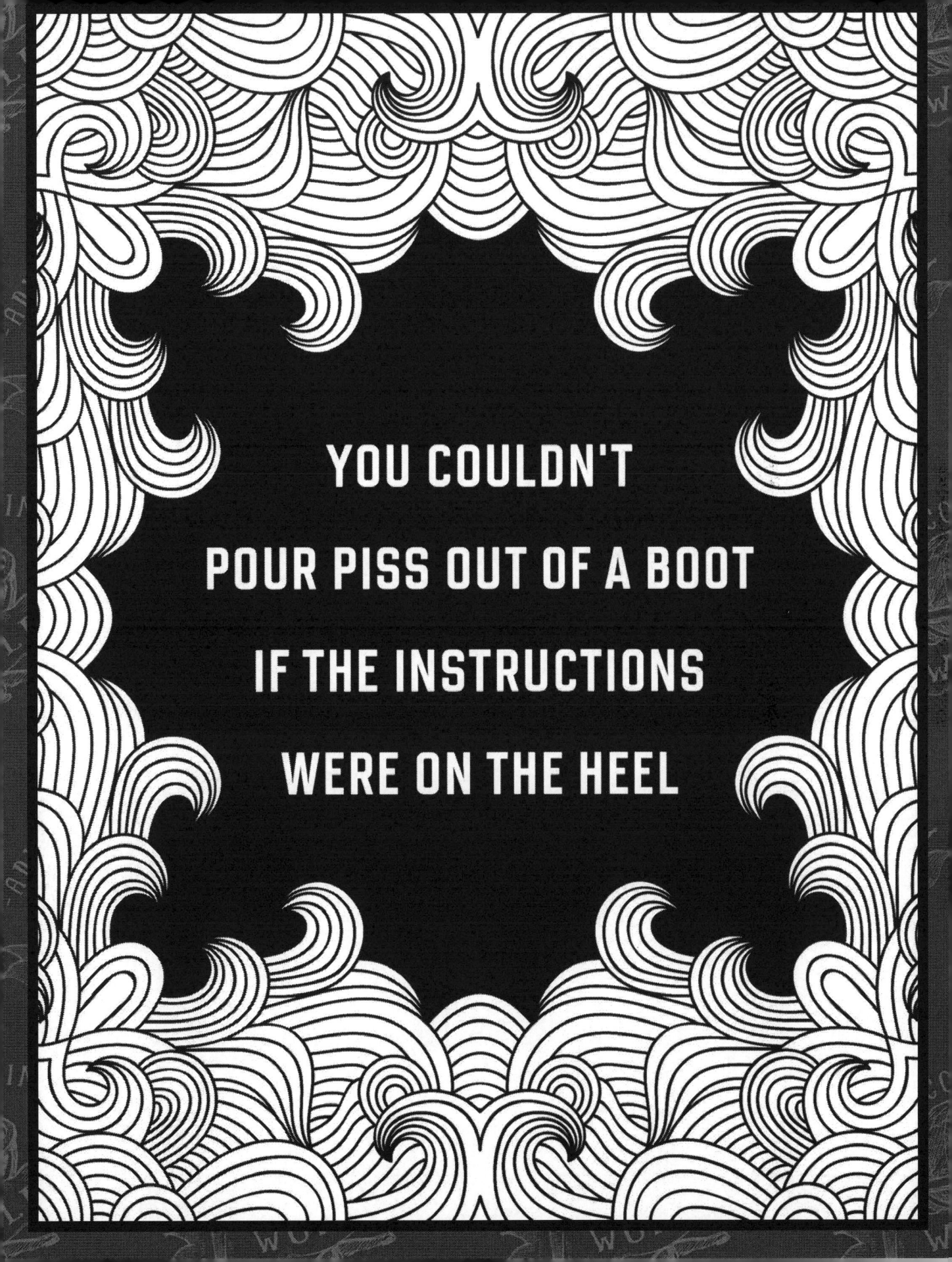

POUR PISS OUT OF A BOOT

IF THE INSTRUCTIONS

WERE ON THE HEEL

I'M NOT SAYING I HATE YOU BUT

I WOULD UNPLUG YOUR LIFE SUPPORT TO CHARGE MY FUCKING PHONE

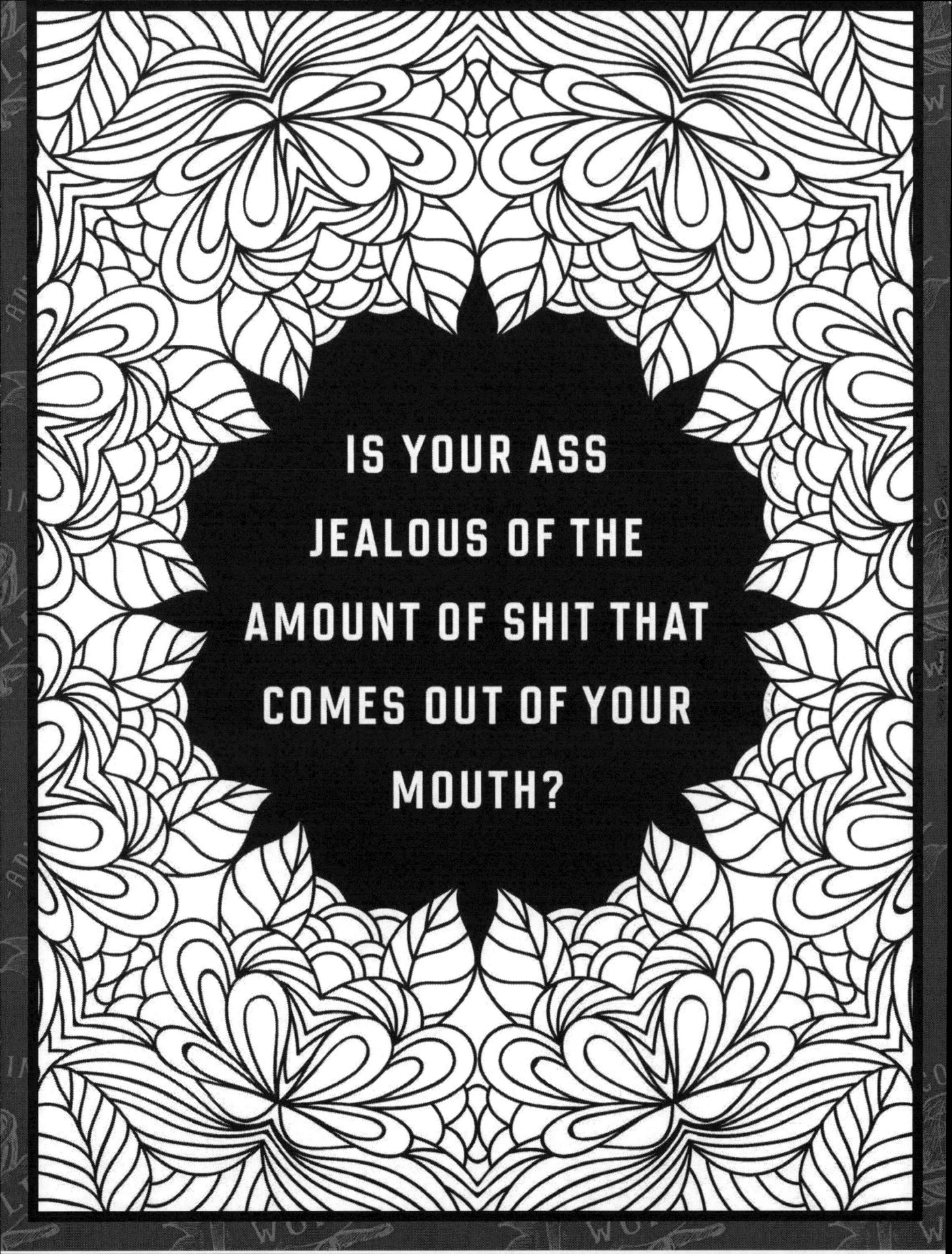

IS YOUR ASS JEALOUS OF THE AMOUNT OF SHIT THAT COMES OUT OF YOUR MOUTH?

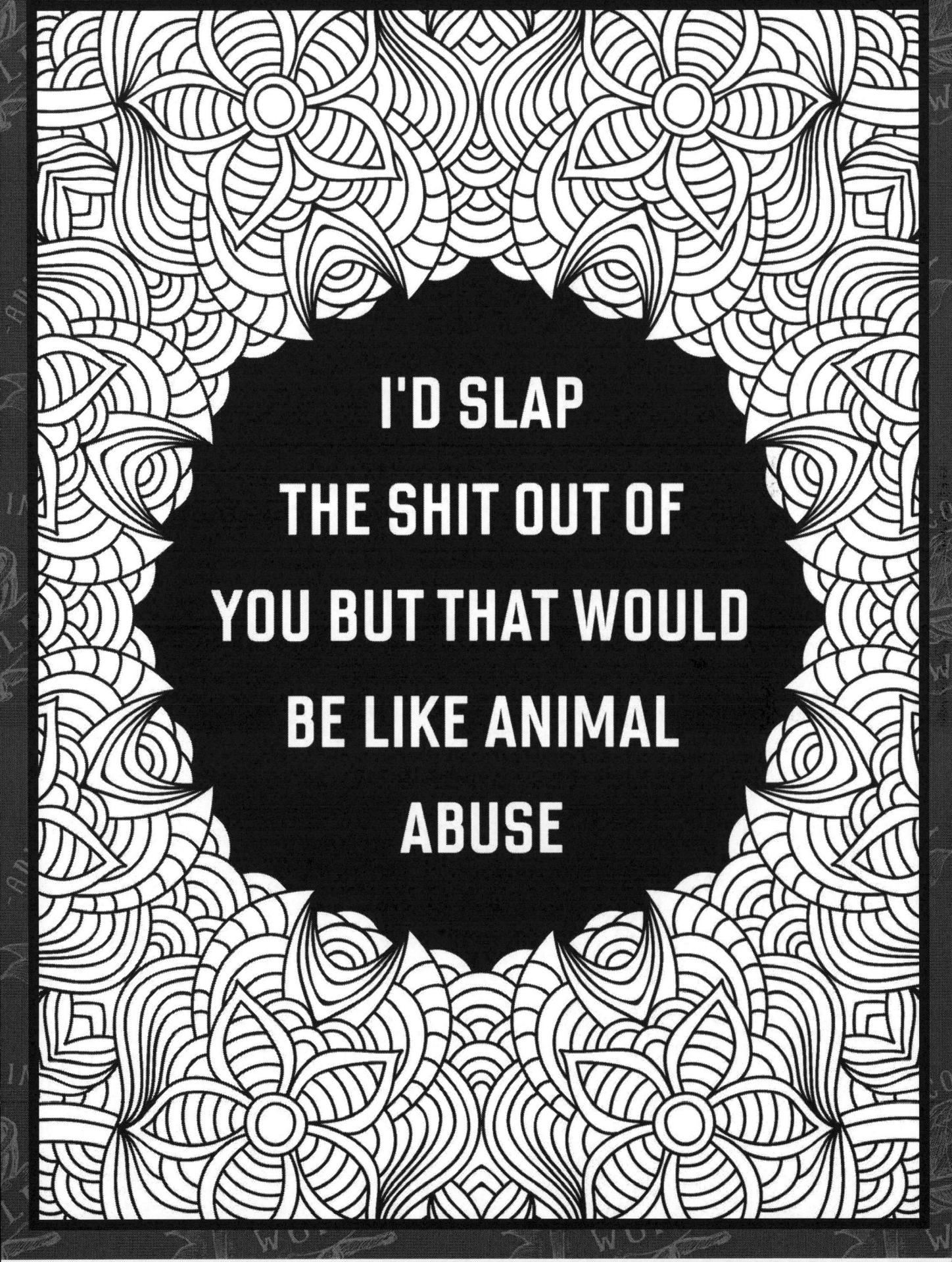

I'D SLAP THE SHIT OUT OF YOU BUT THAT WOULD BE LIKE ANIMAL ABUSE

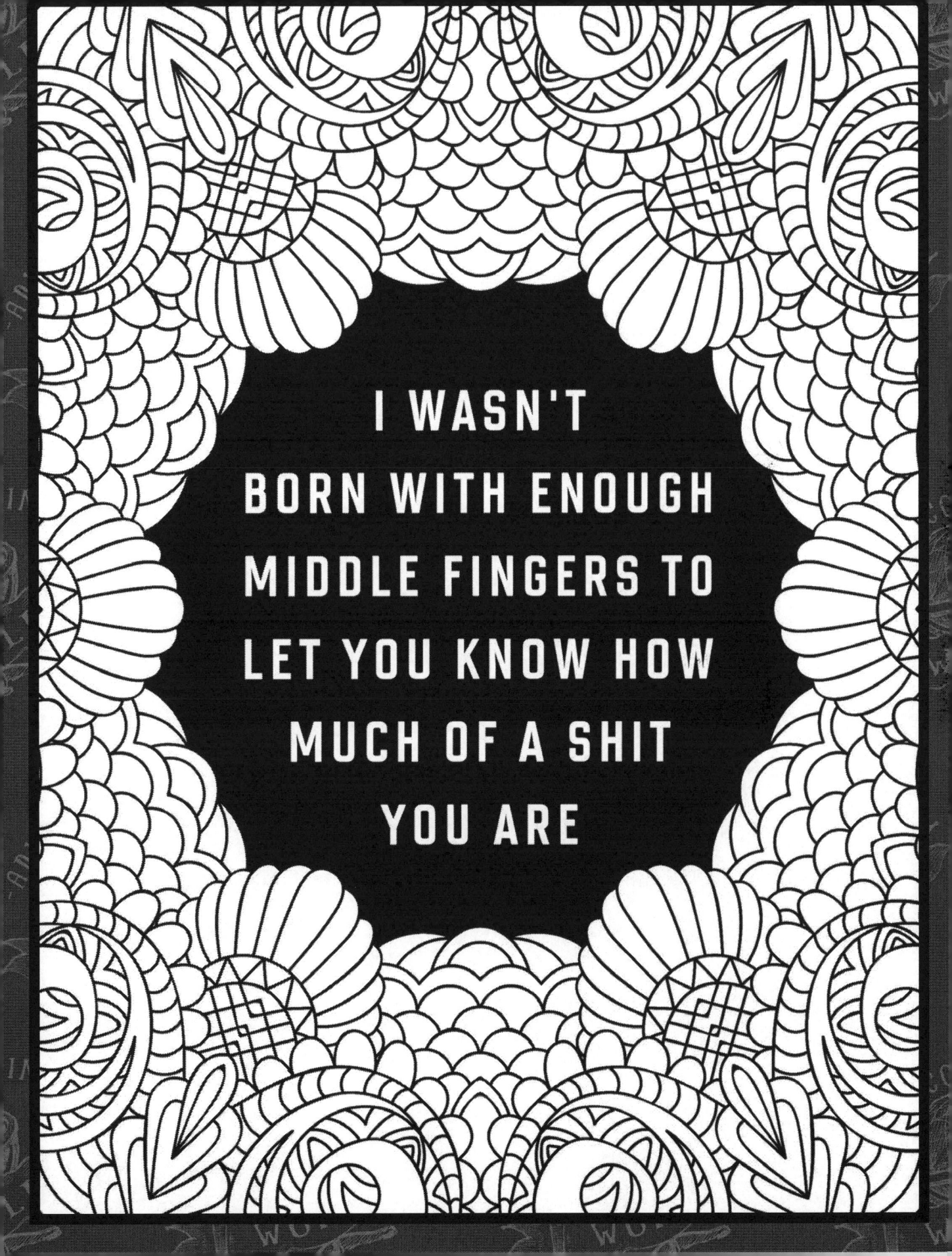

I WASN'T BORN WITH ENOUGH MIDDLE FINGERS TO LET YOU KNOW HOW MUCH OF A SHIT YOU ARE

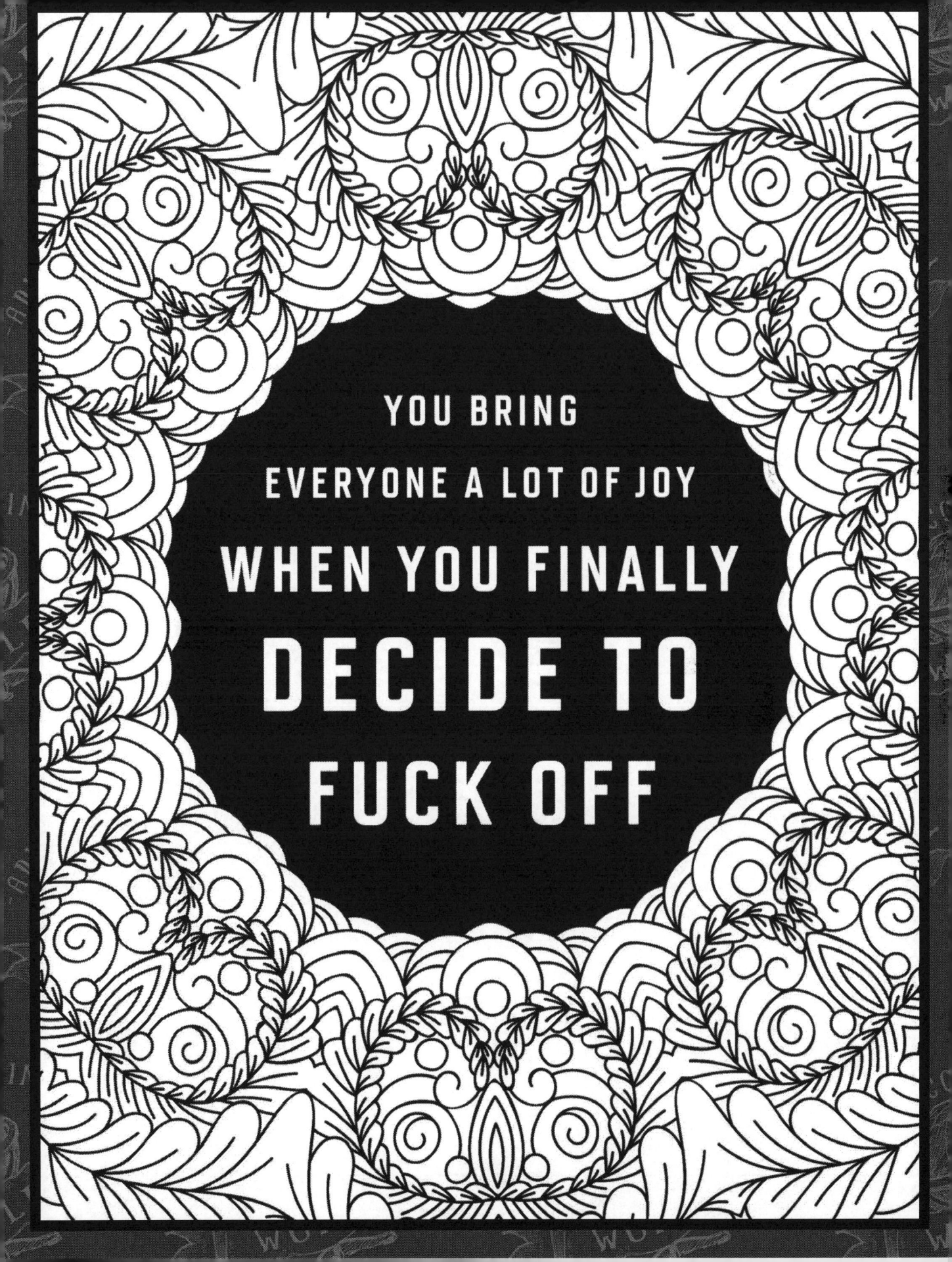

YOU BRING EVERYONE A LOT OF JOY WHEN YOU FINALLY **DECIDE TO FUCK OFF**

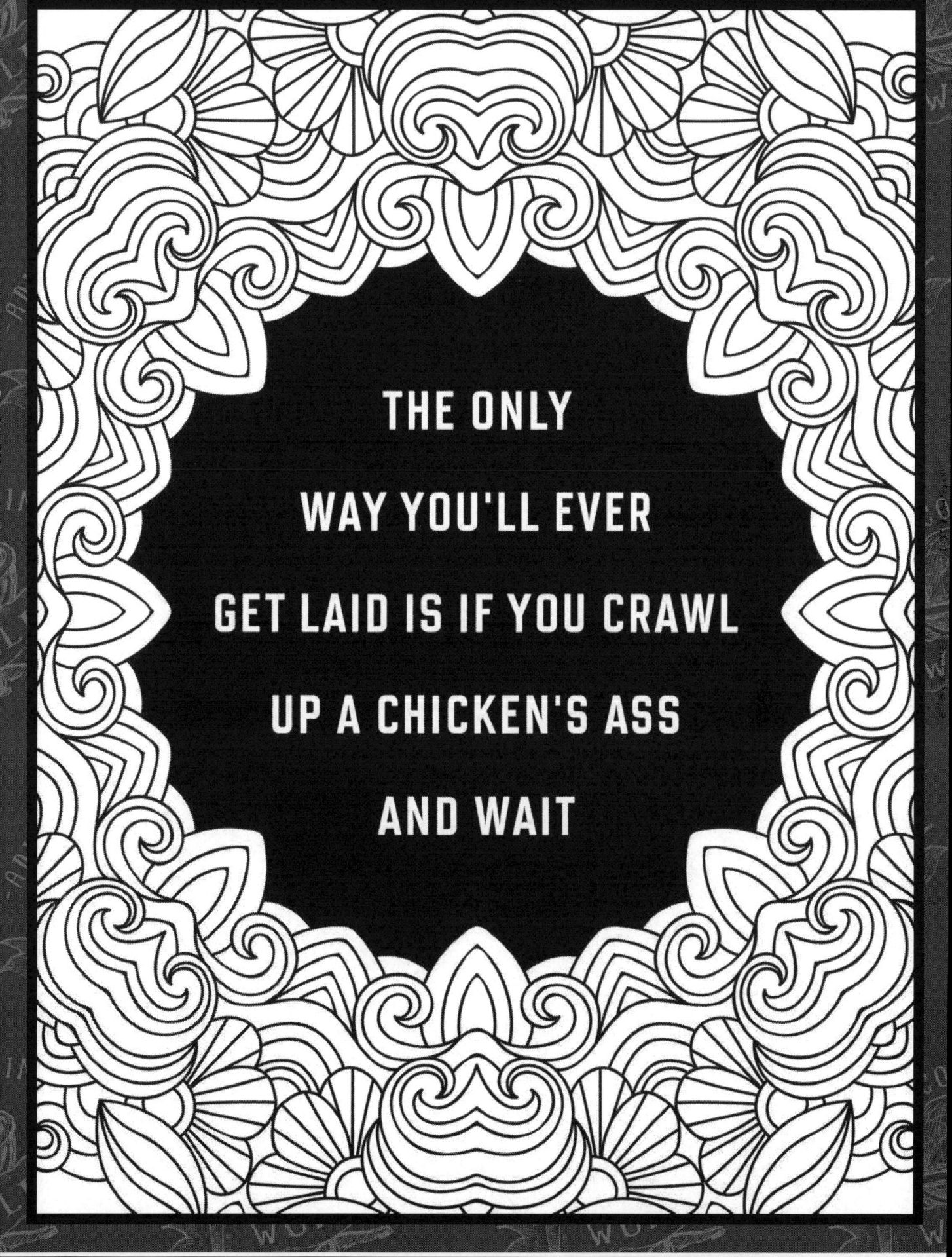

THE ONLY WAY YOU'LL EVER GET LAID IS IF YOU CRAWL UP A CHICKEN'S ASS AND WAIT

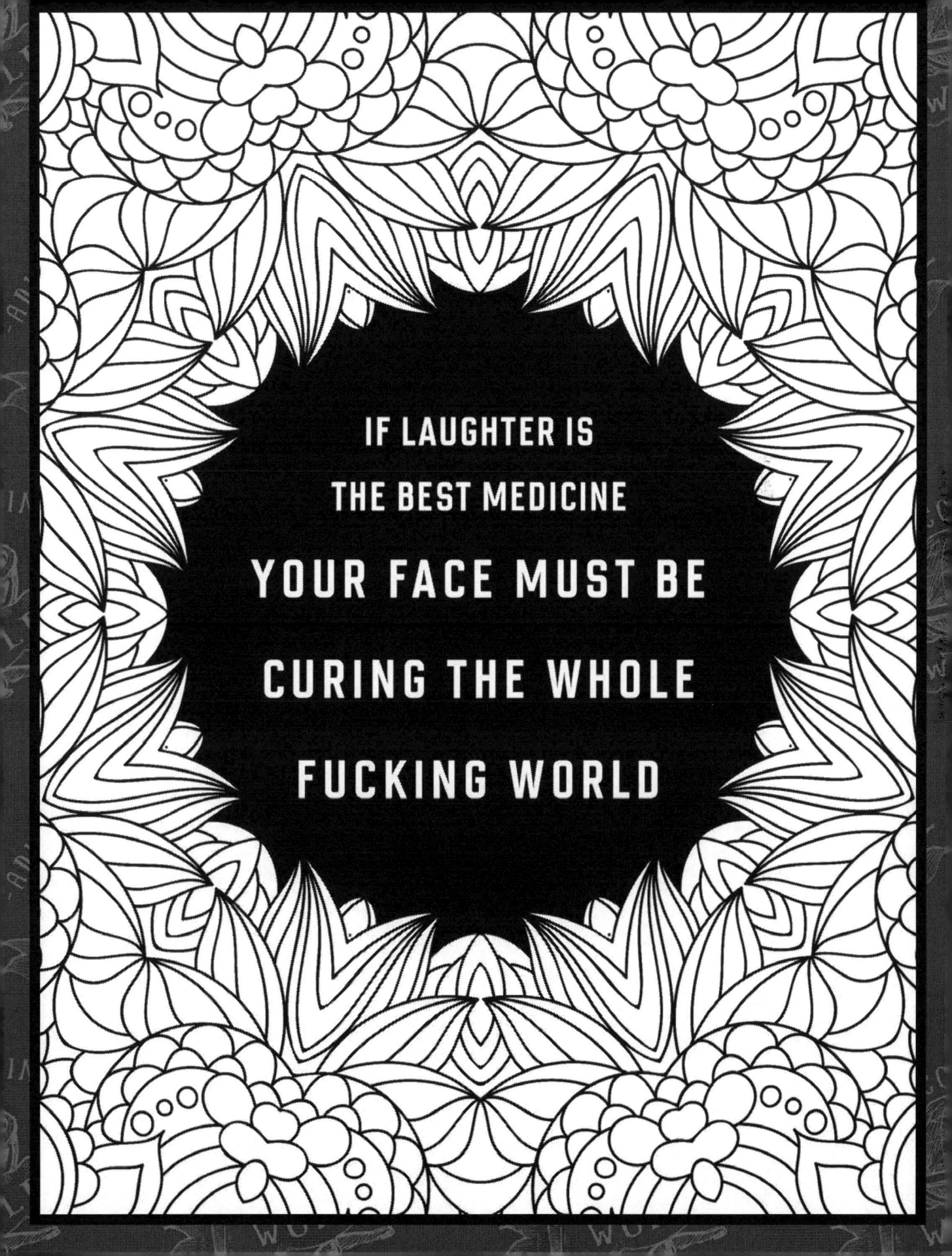

IF LAUGHTER IS
THE BEST MEDICINE
YOUR FACE MUST BE
CURING THE WHOLE
FUCKING WORLD

FUCK YOU YOU FUCKING FUCK

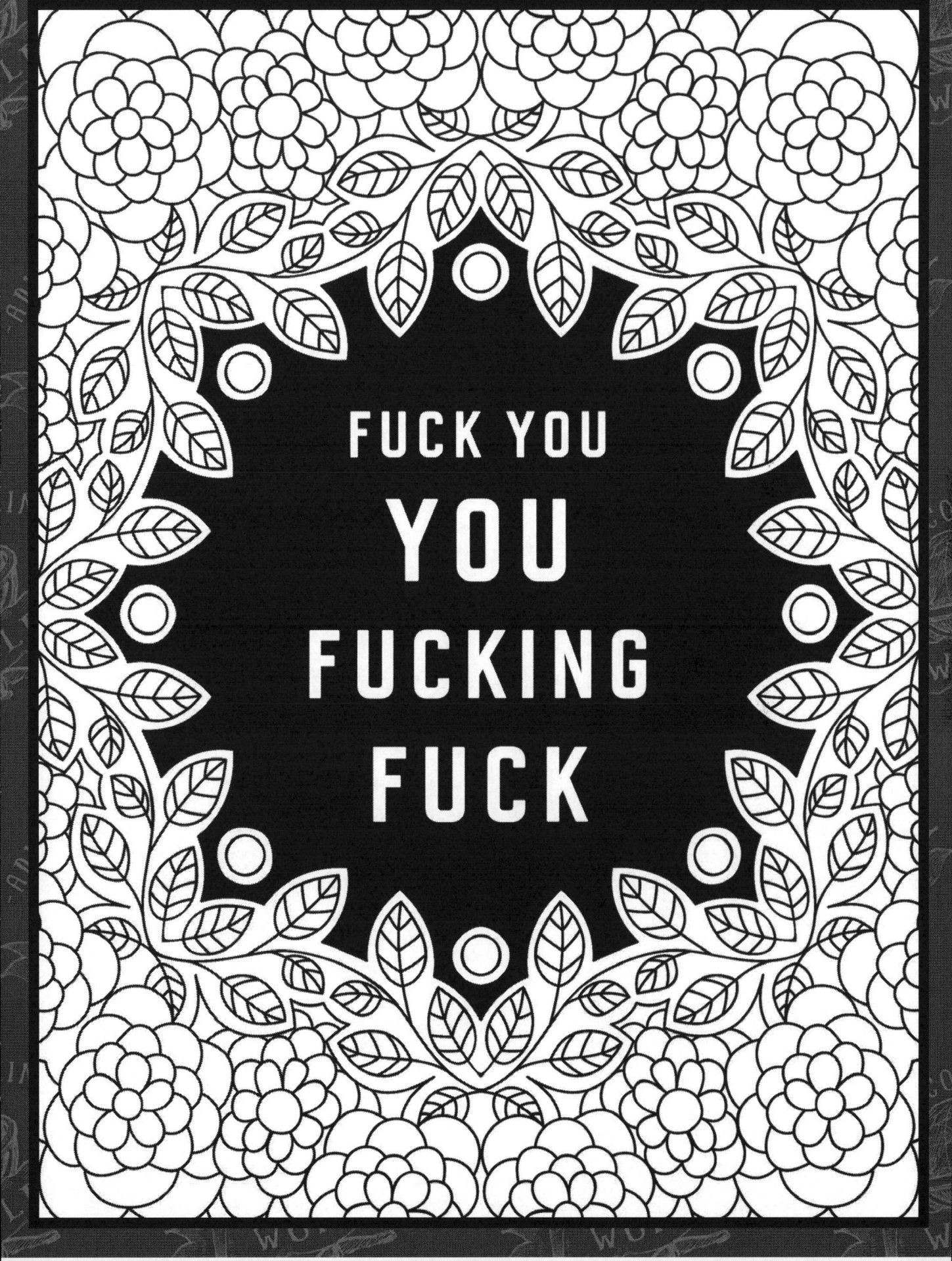

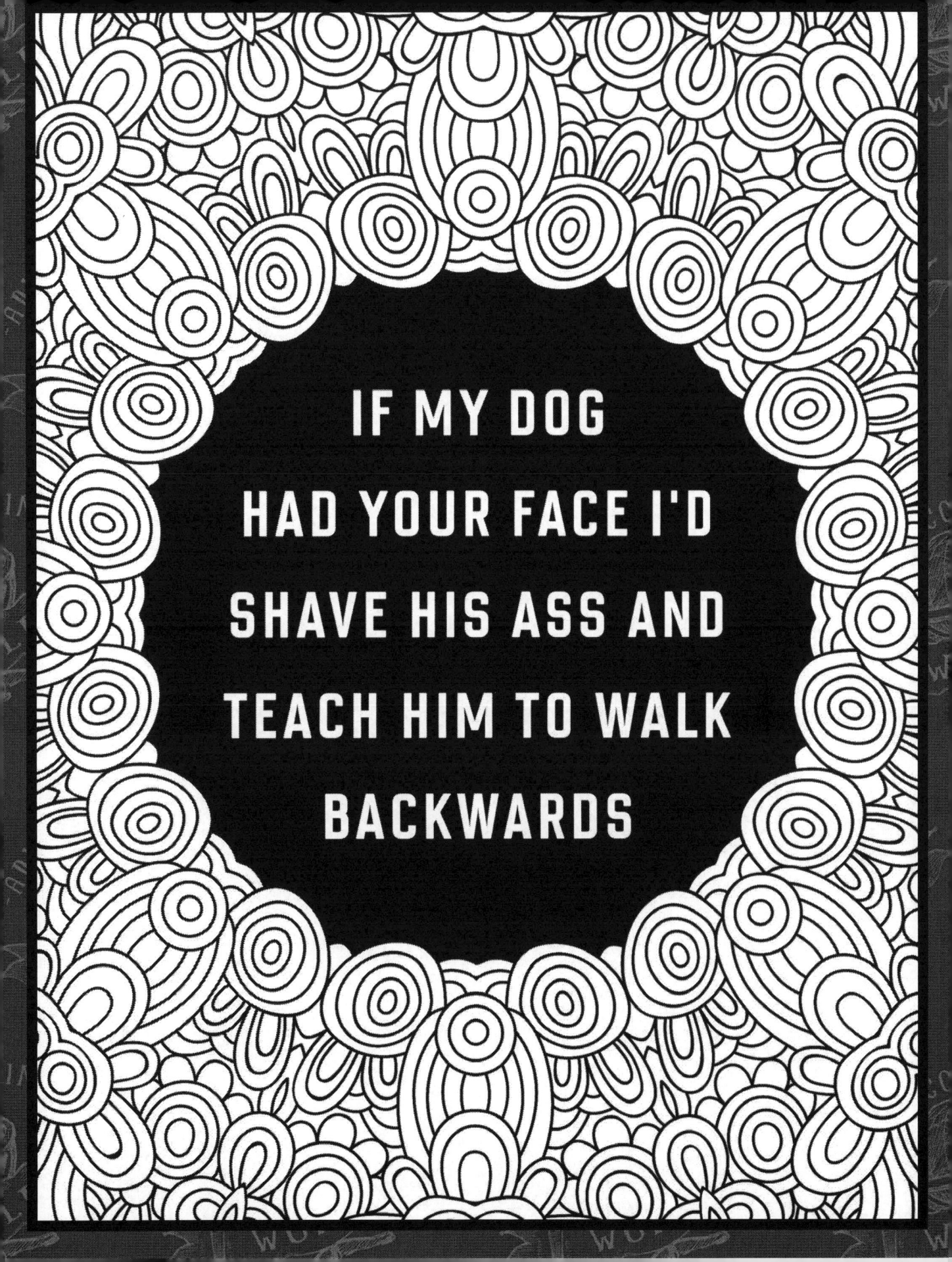

IF MY DOG HAD YOUR FACE I'D SHAVE HIS ASS AND TEACH HIM TO WALK BACKWARDS

IT'S CALLED FUCK OFF AND IT'S LOCATED OVER THERE

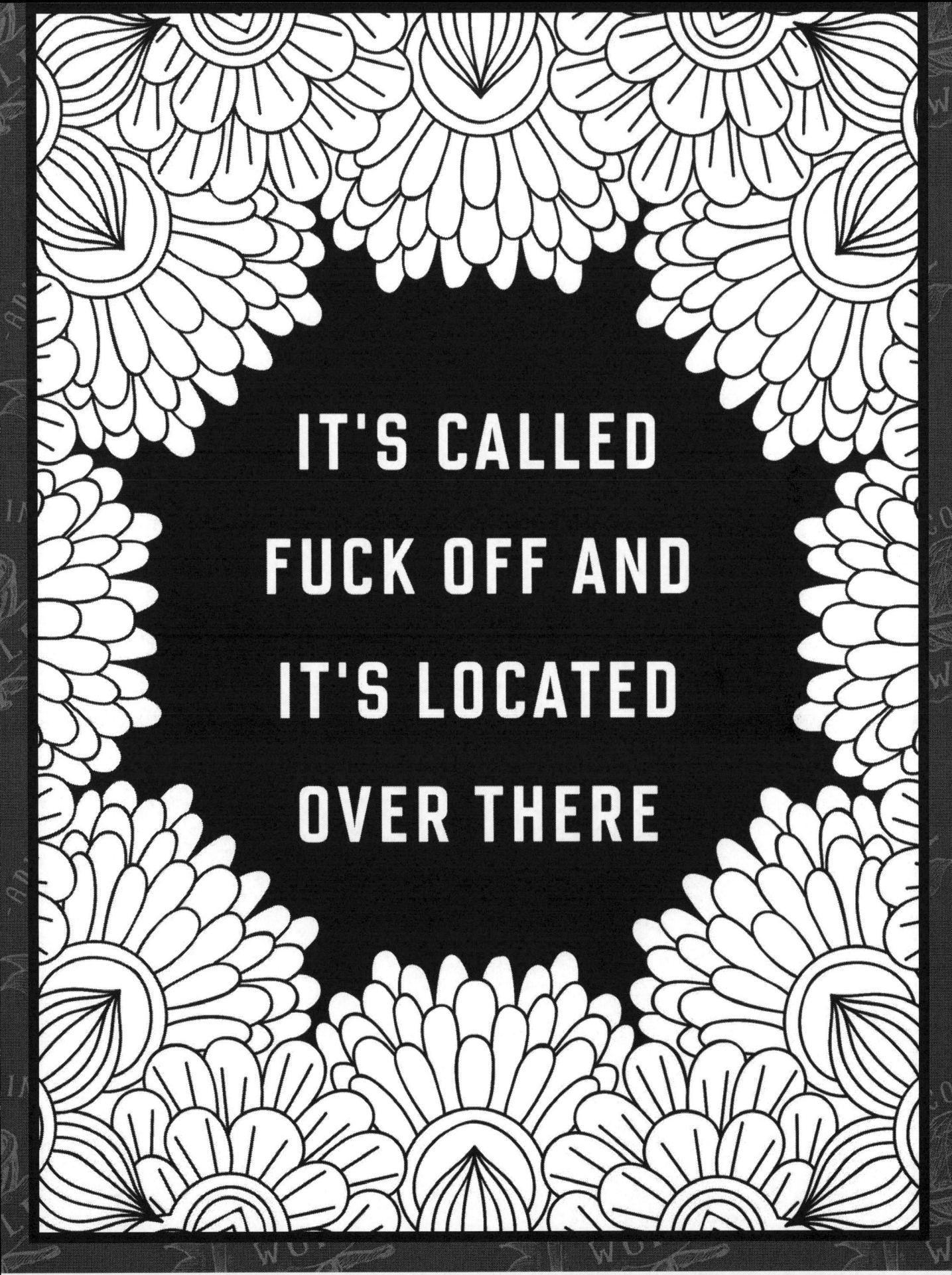

YOU HAVE A HUGE ZIT ON YOUR NECK

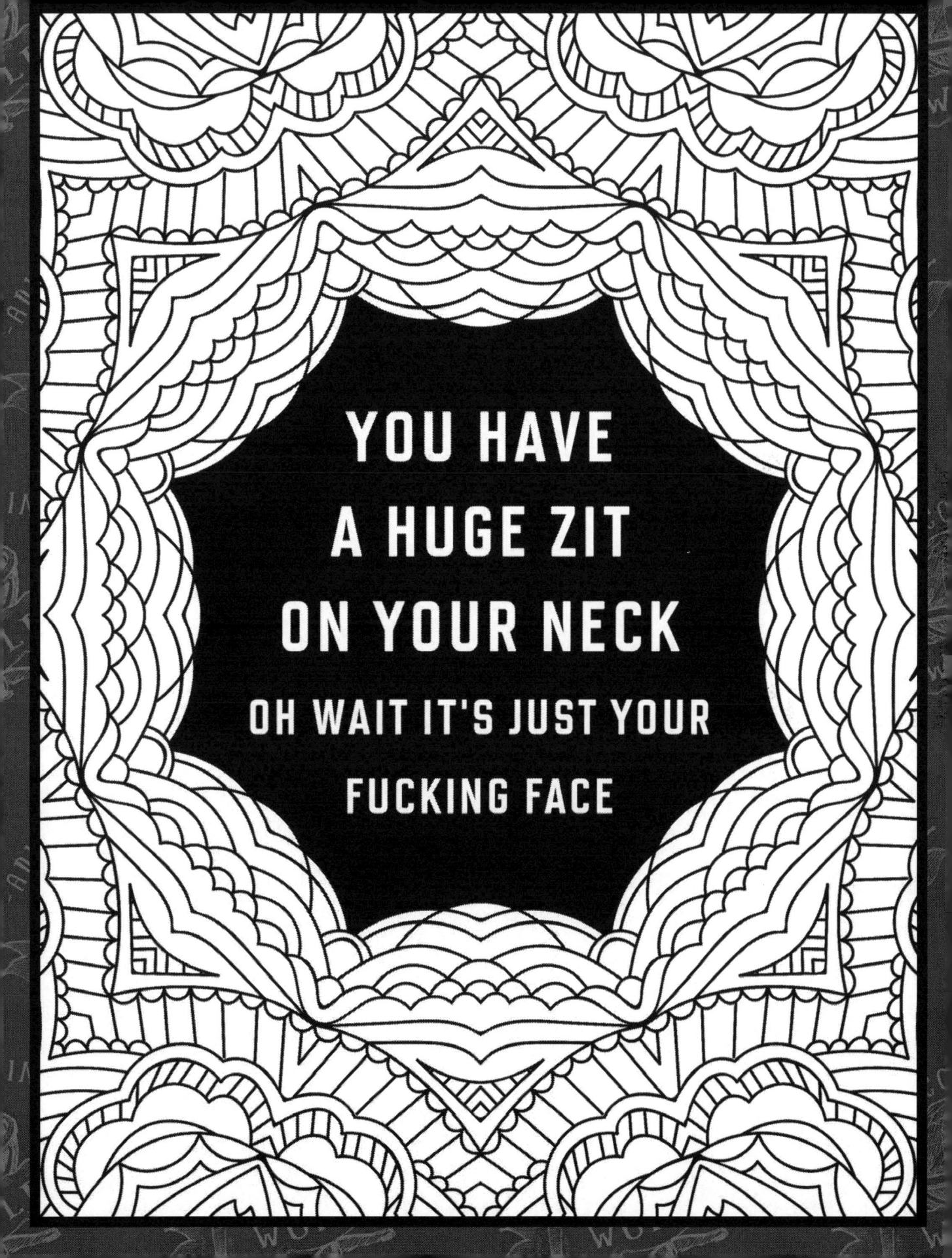

OH WAIT IT'S JUST YOUR FUCKING FACE

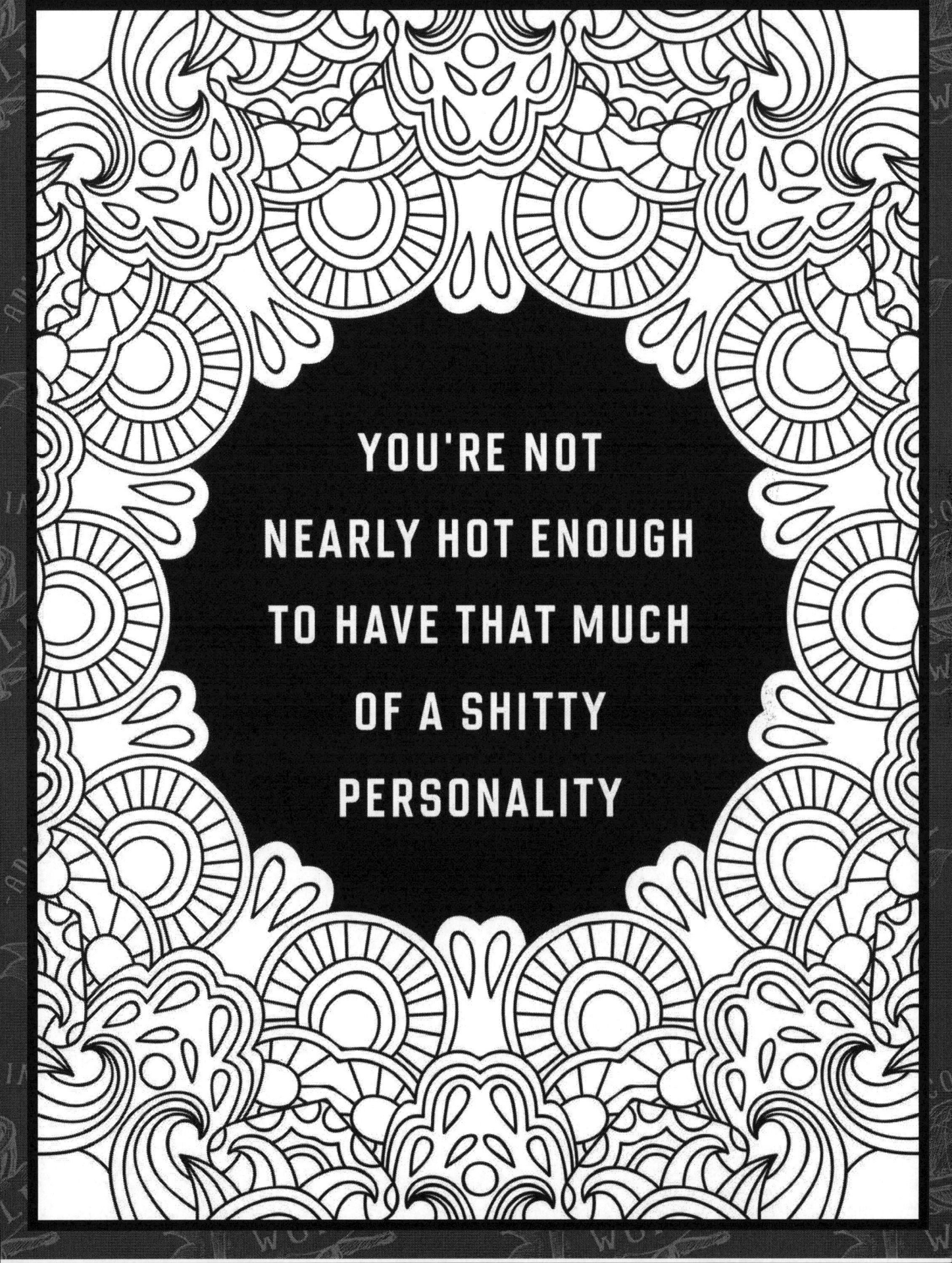

YOU'RE NOT NEARLY HOT ENOUGH TO HAVE THAT MUCH OF A SHITTY PERSONALITY

YOUR MOTHER SHOULD HAVE FUCKING SWALLOWED YOU

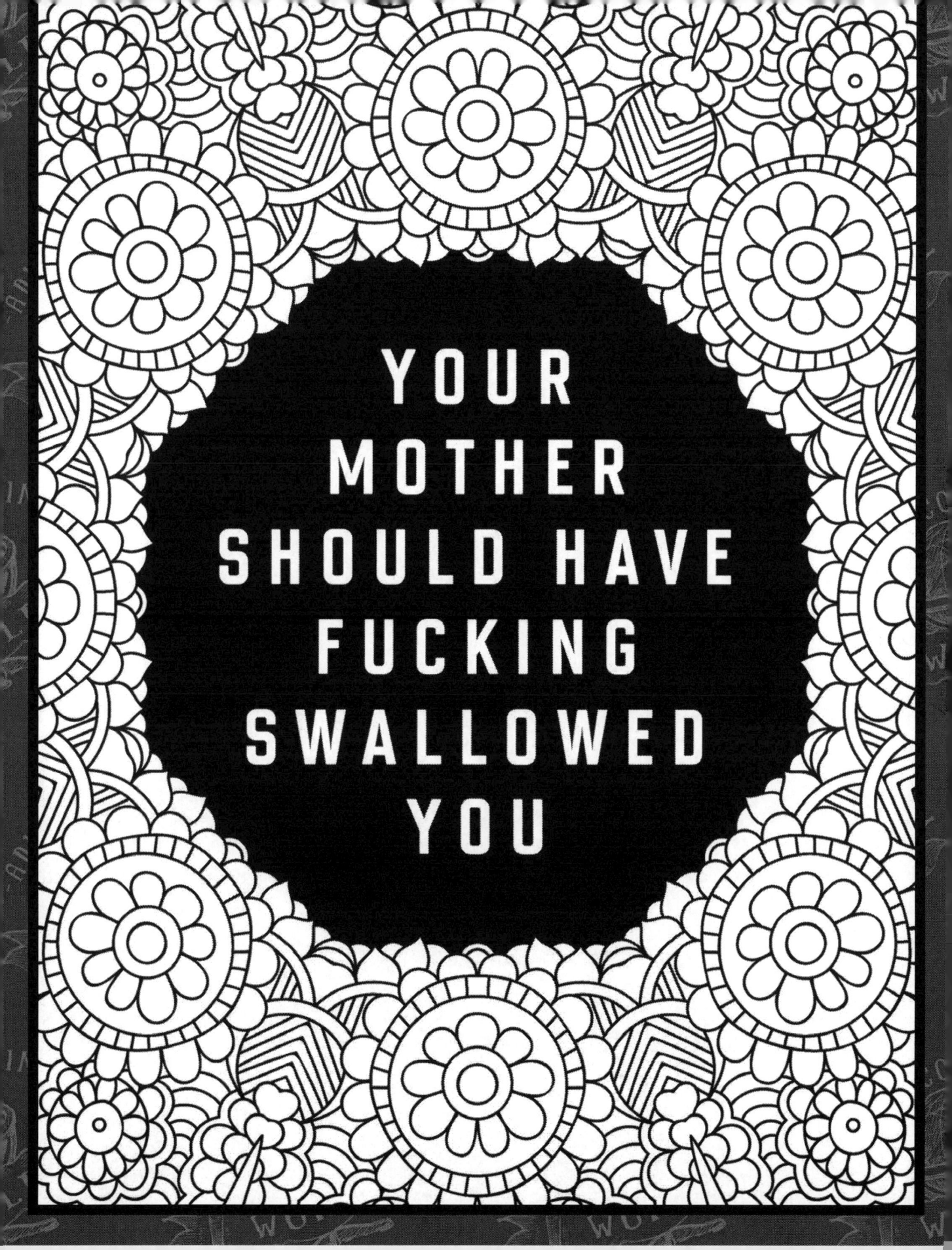

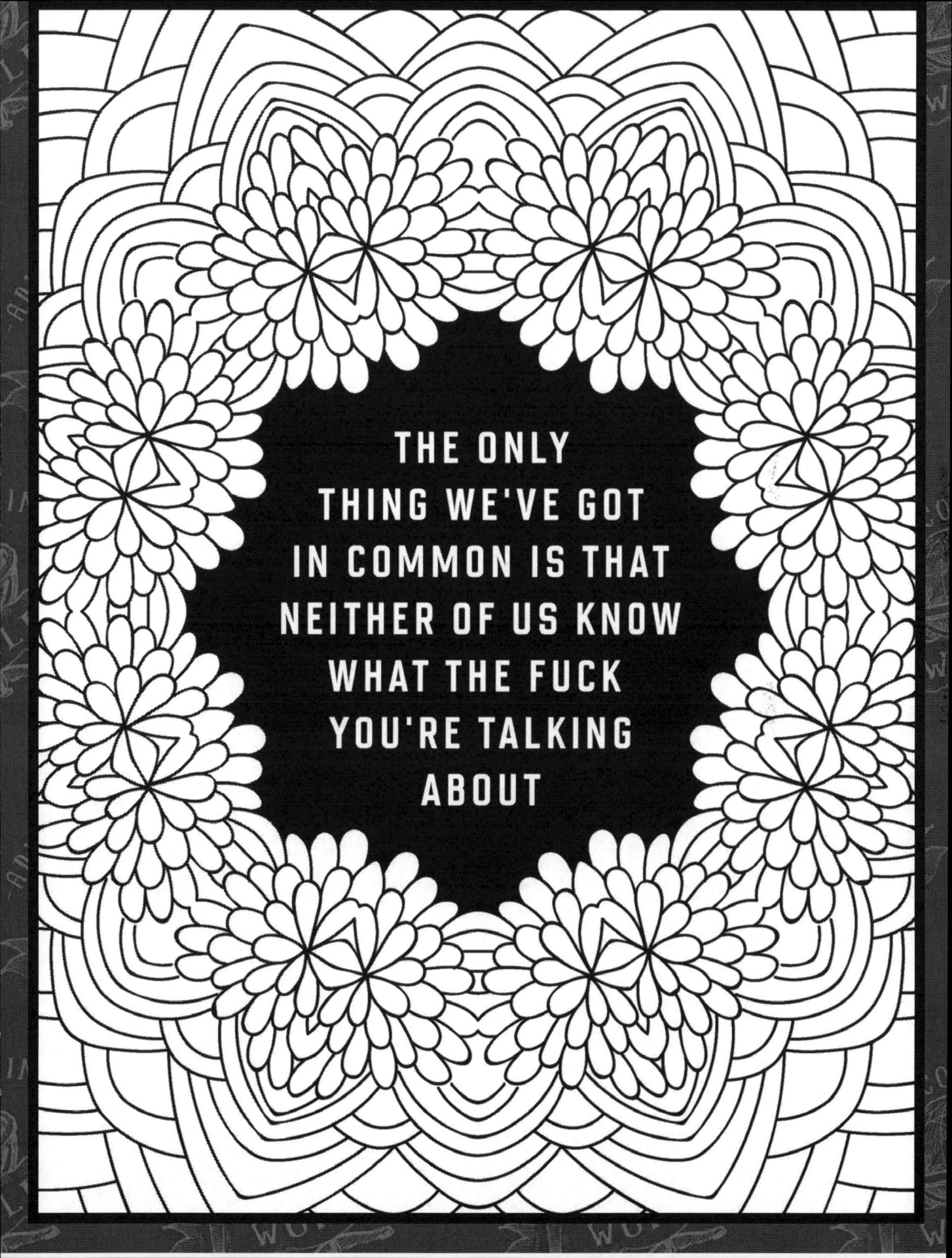

THE ONLY THING WE'VE GOT IN COMMON IS THAT NEITHER OF US KNOW WHAT THE FUCK YOU'RE TALKING ABOUT

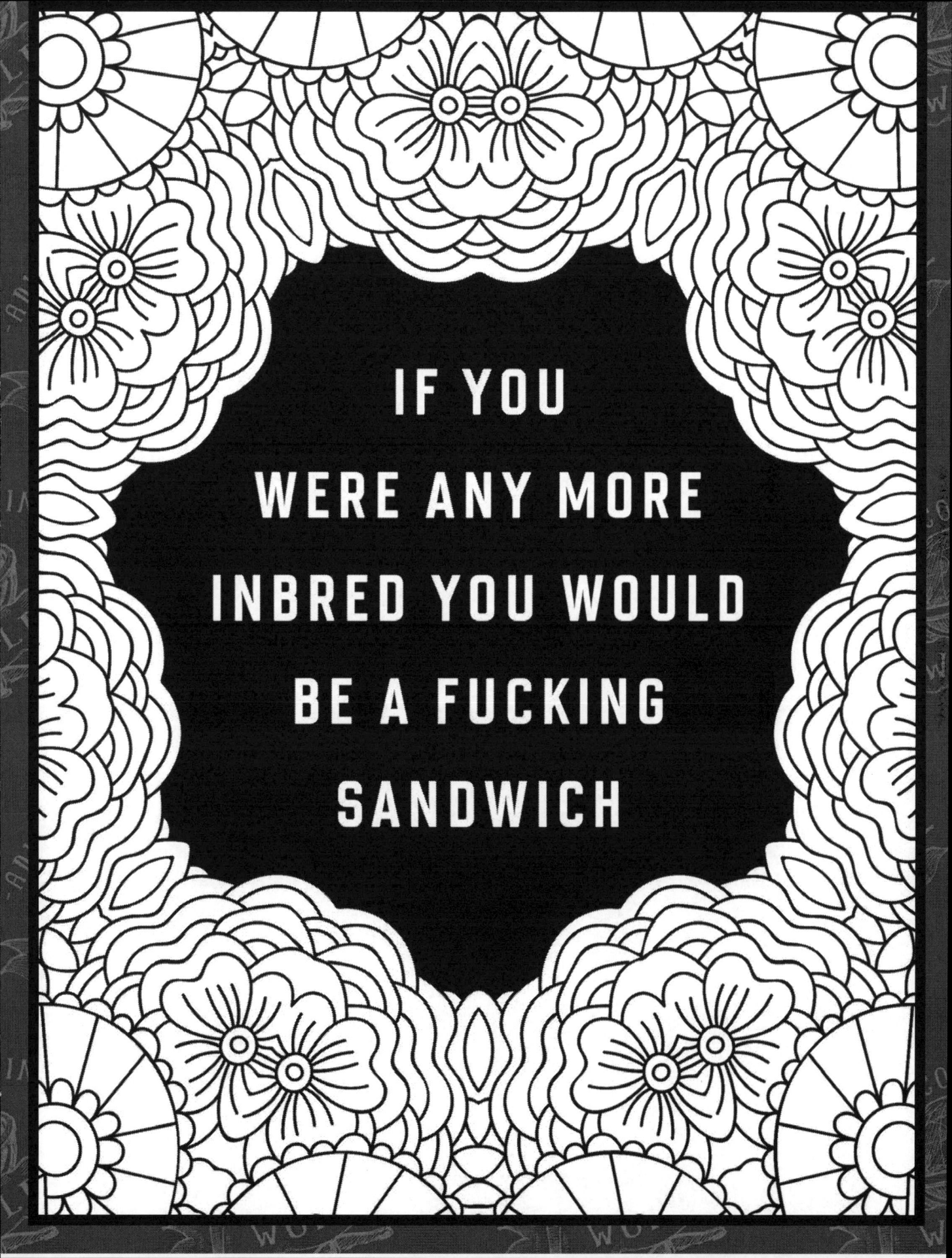

IF YOU WERE ANY MORE INBRED YOU WOULD BE A FUCKING SANDWICH

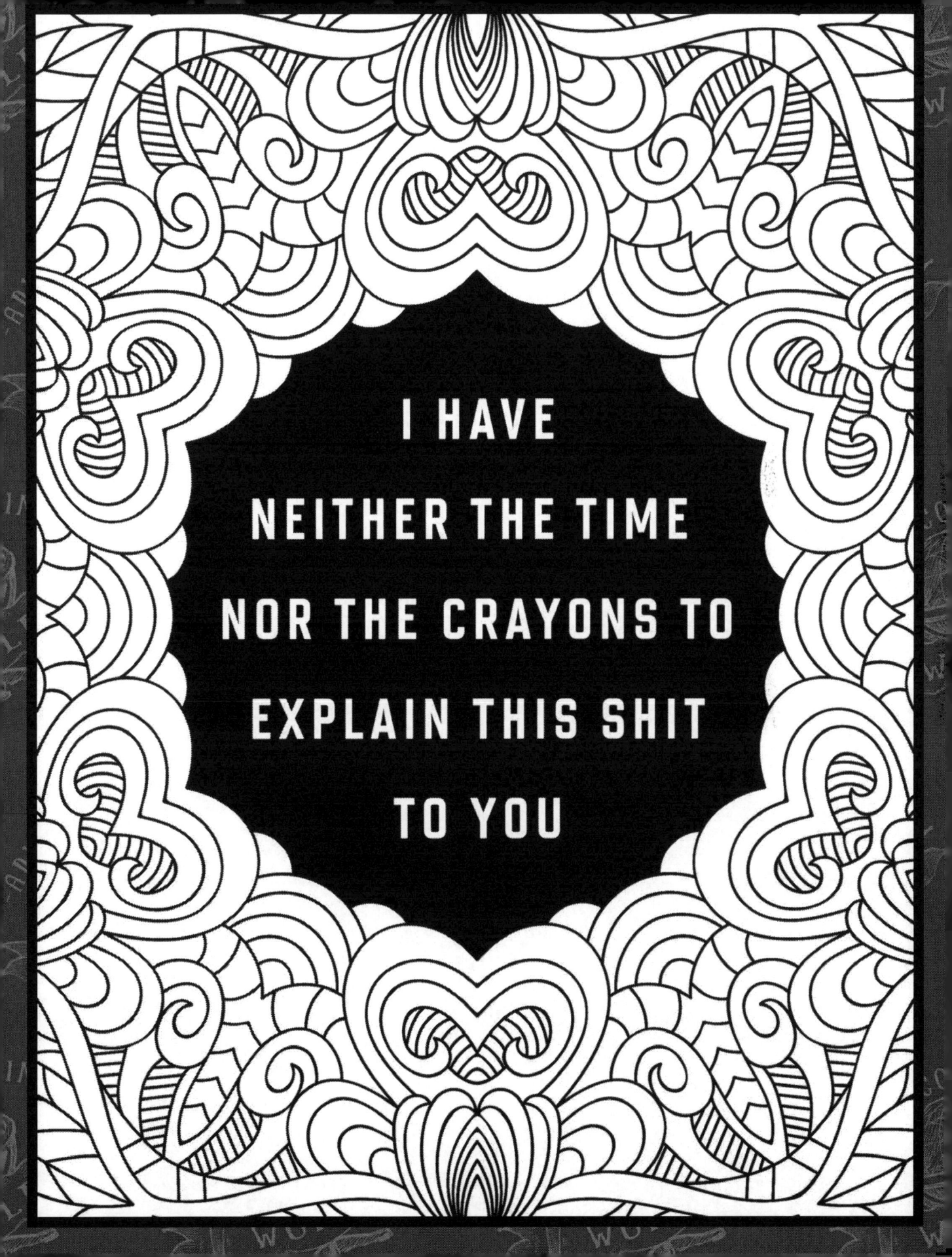

I HAVE NEITHER THE TIME NOR THE CRAYONS TO EXPLAIN THIS SHIT TO YOU

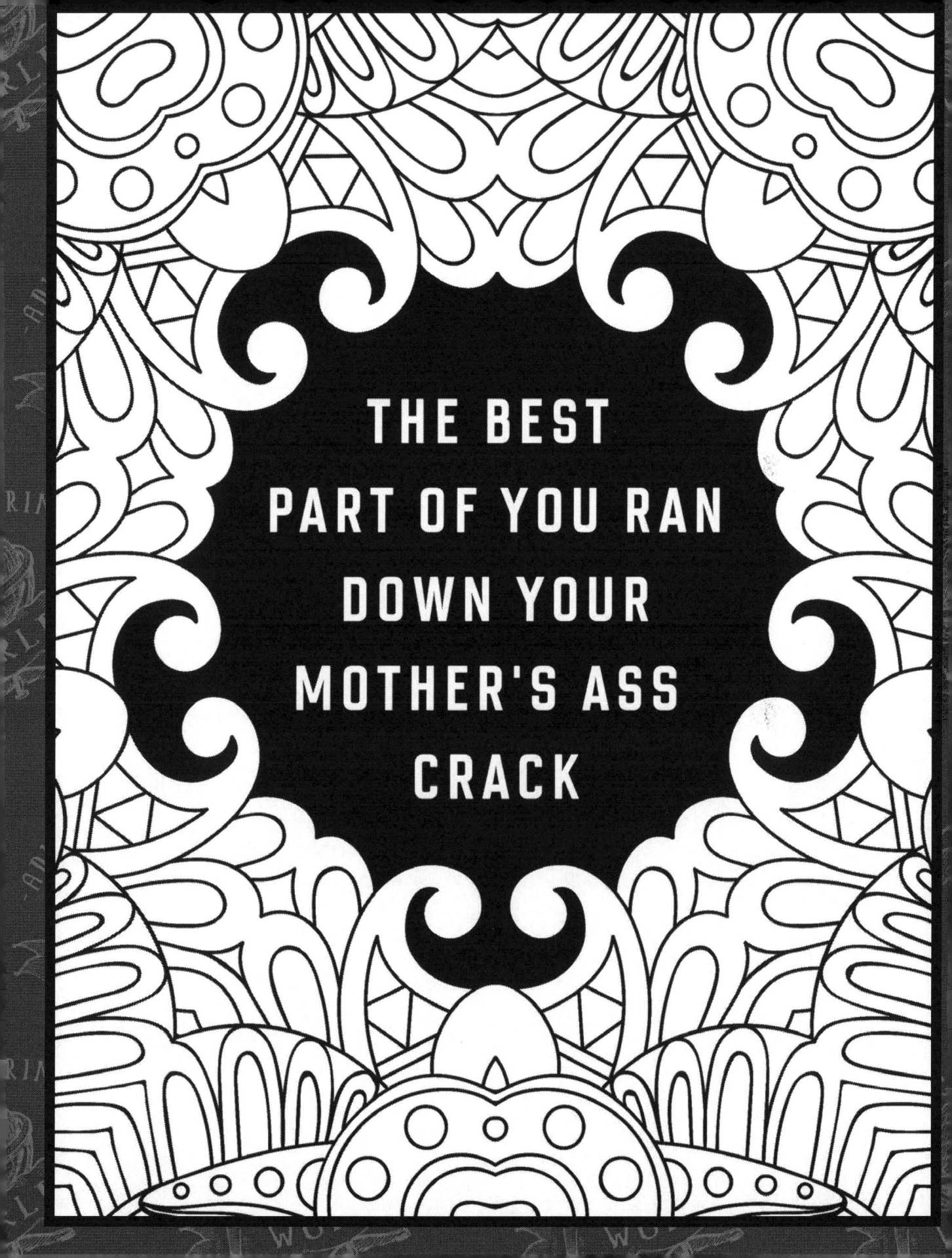

THE BEST PART OF YOU RAN DOWN YOUR MOTHER'S ASS CRACK

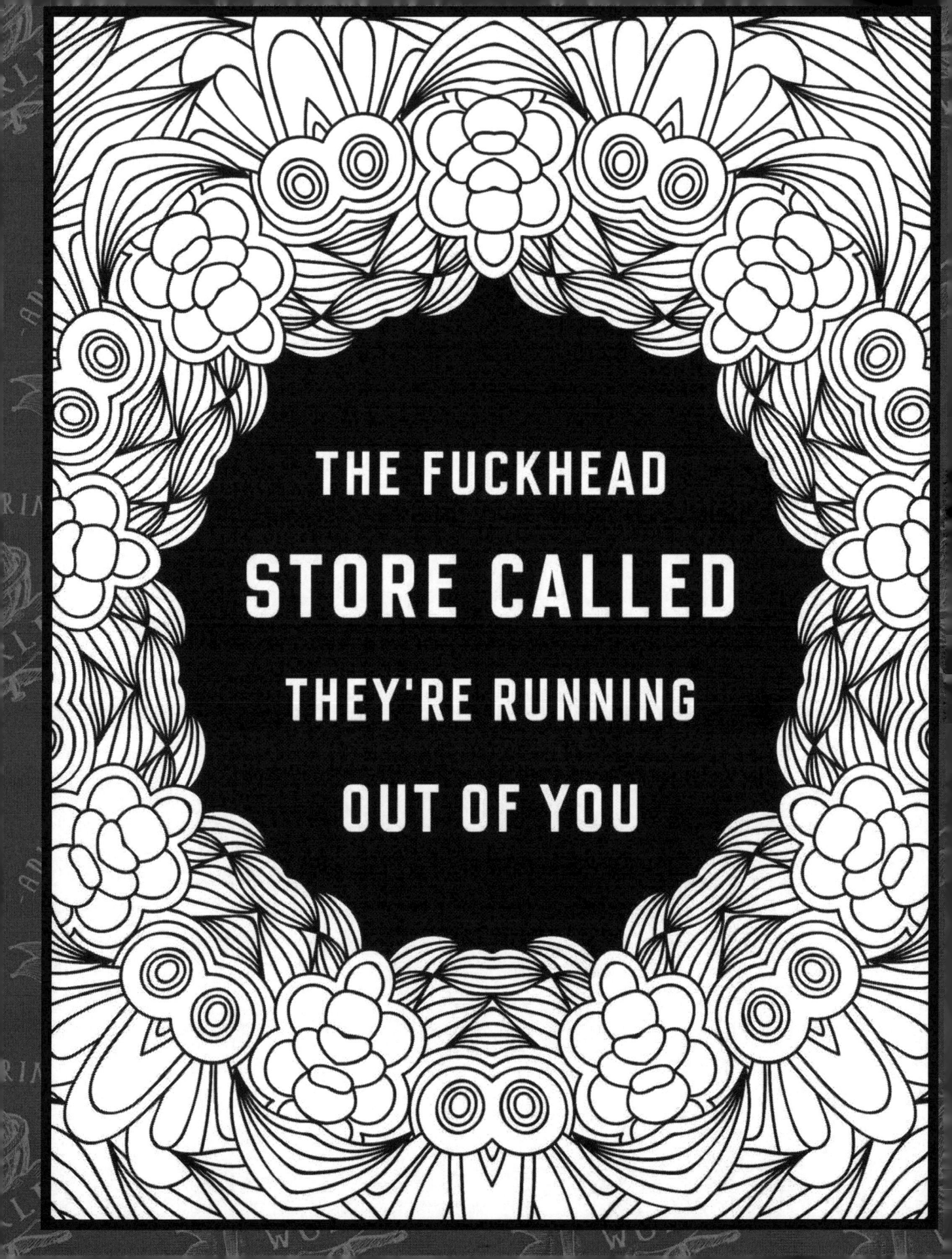

THE FUCKHEAD STORE CALLED THEY'RE RUNNING OUT OF YOU

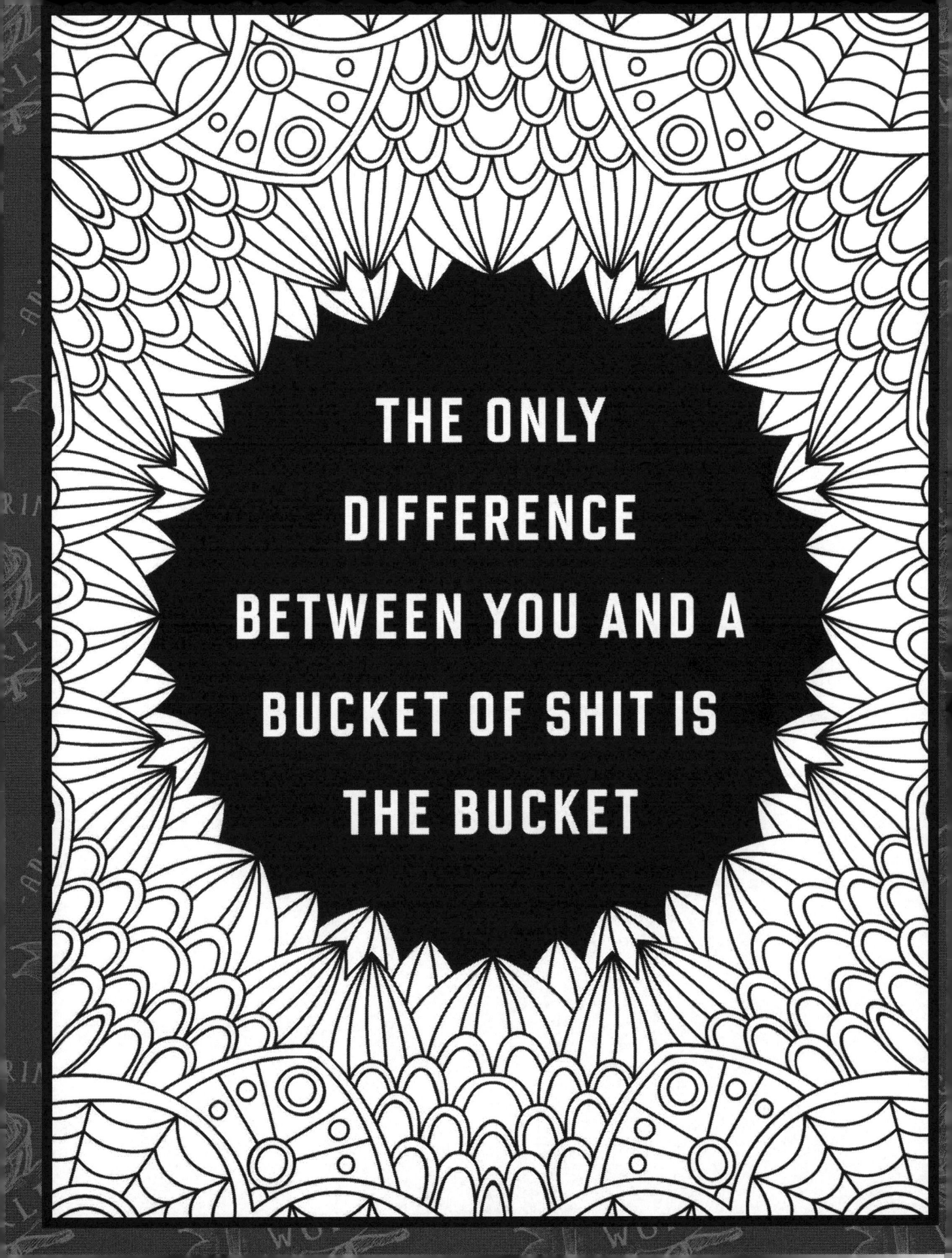

THE ONLY DIFFERENCE BETWEEN YOU AND A BUCKET OF SHIT IS THE BUCKET

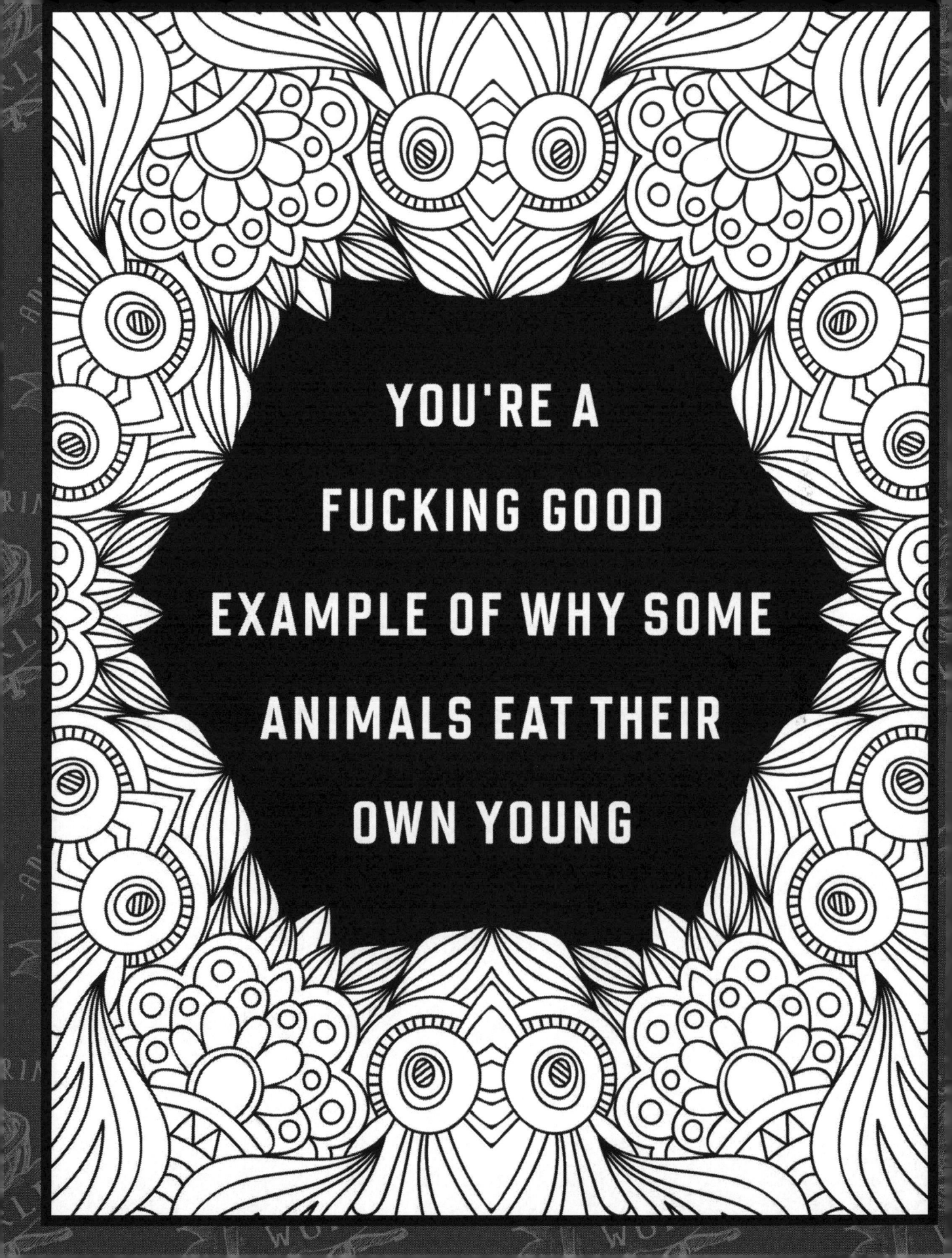

YOU'RE A FUCKING GOOD EXAMPLE OF WHY SOME ANIMALS EAT THEIR OWN YOUNG

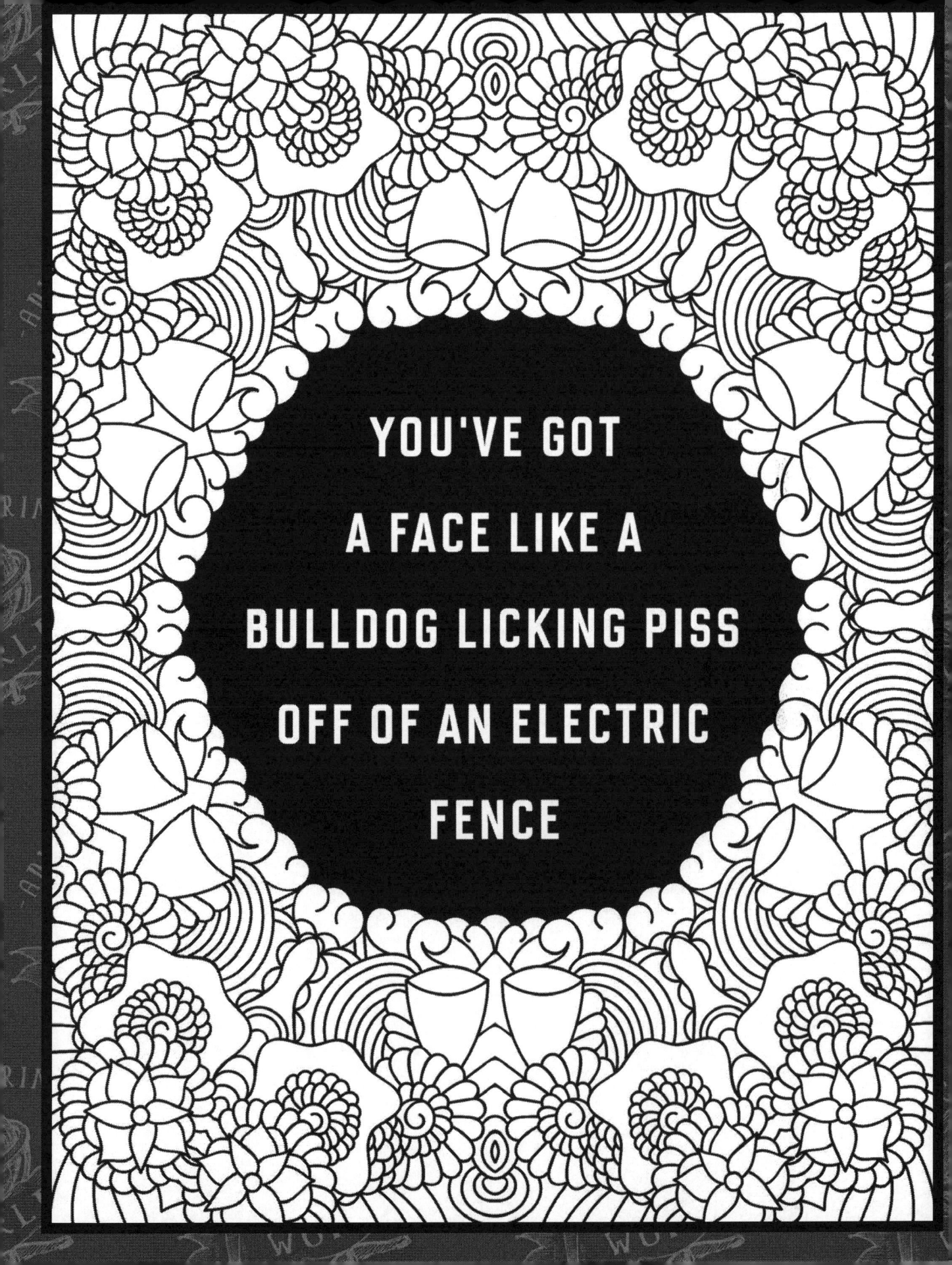

YOU'VE GOT A FACE LIKE A BULLDOG LICKING PISS OFF OF AN ELECTRIC FENCE

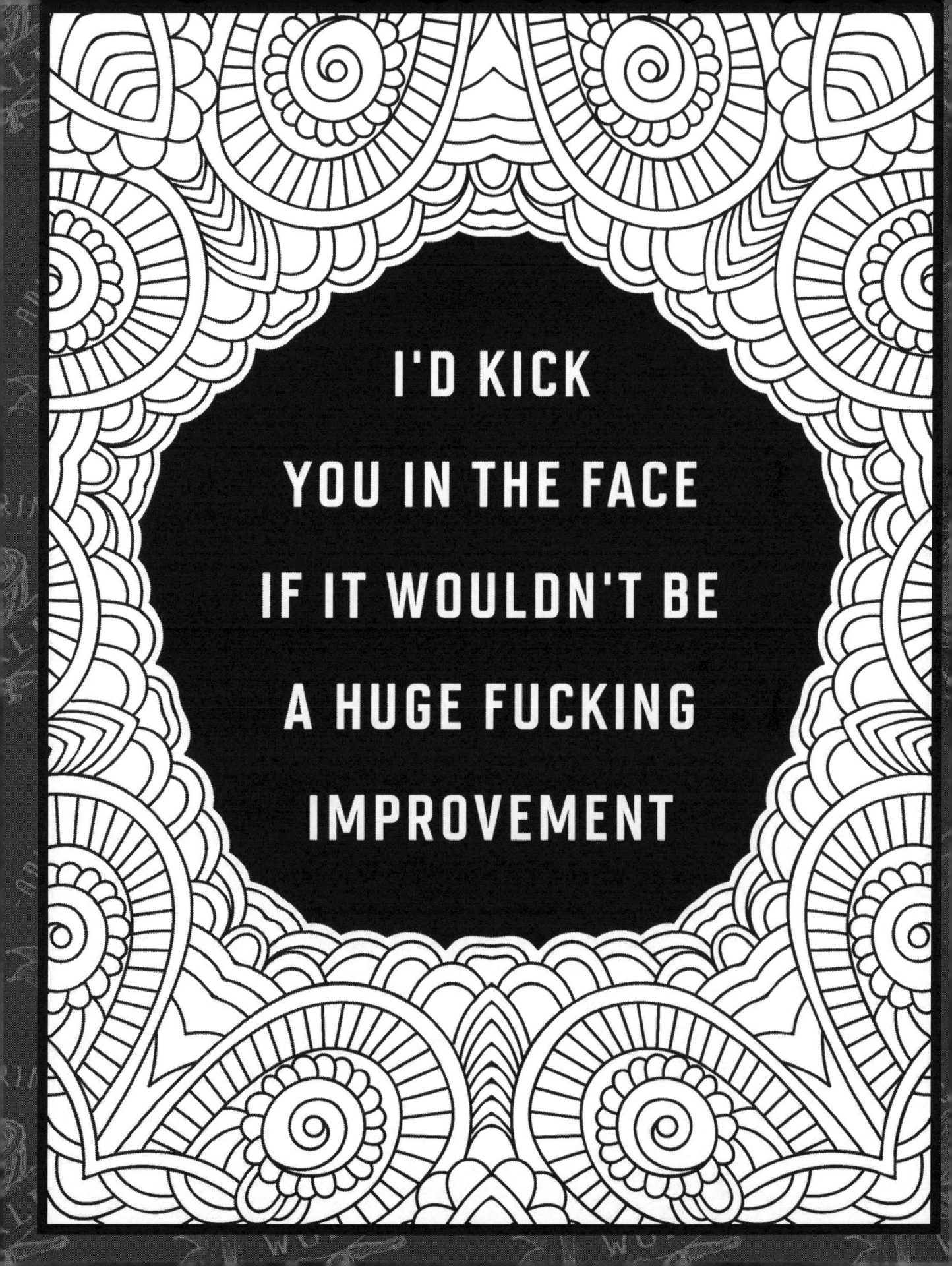

I'D KICK YOU IN THE FACE IF IT WOULDN'T BE A HUGE FUCKING IMPROVEMENT

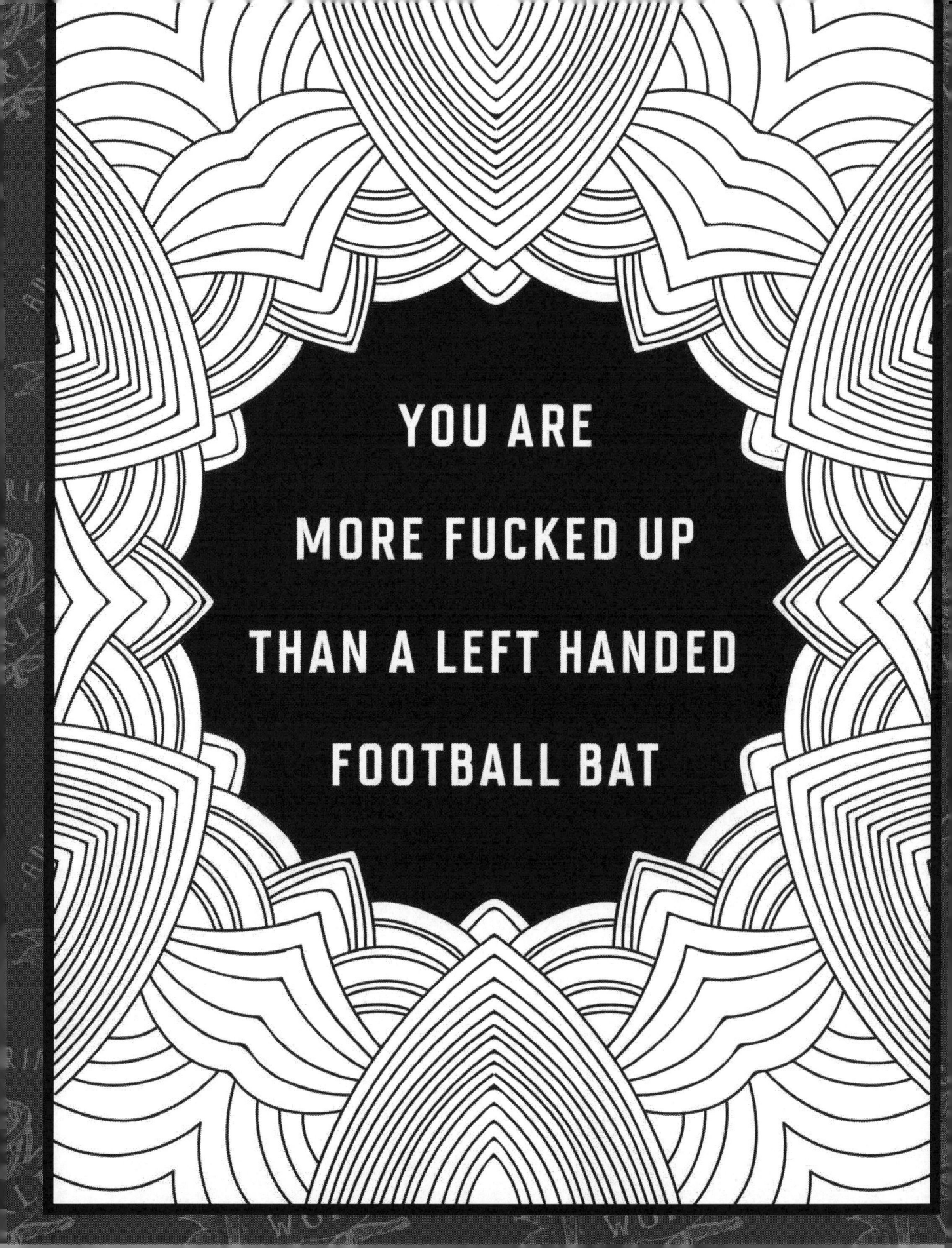

YOU ARE MORE FUCKED UP THAN A LEFT HANDED FOOTBALL BAT

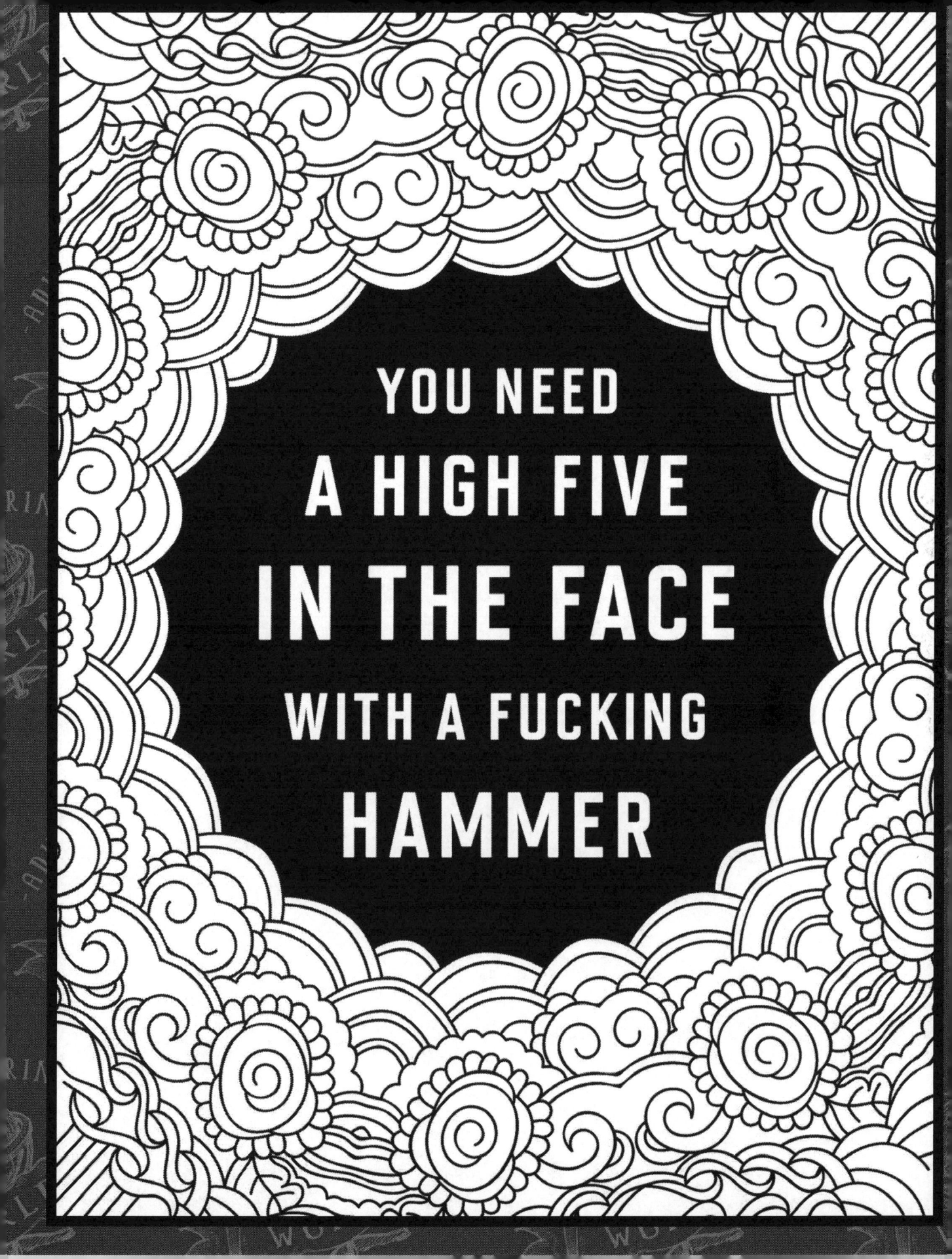

YOU NEED
A HIGH FIVE
IN THE FACE
WITH A FUCKING
HAMMER

CONGRATULATIONS

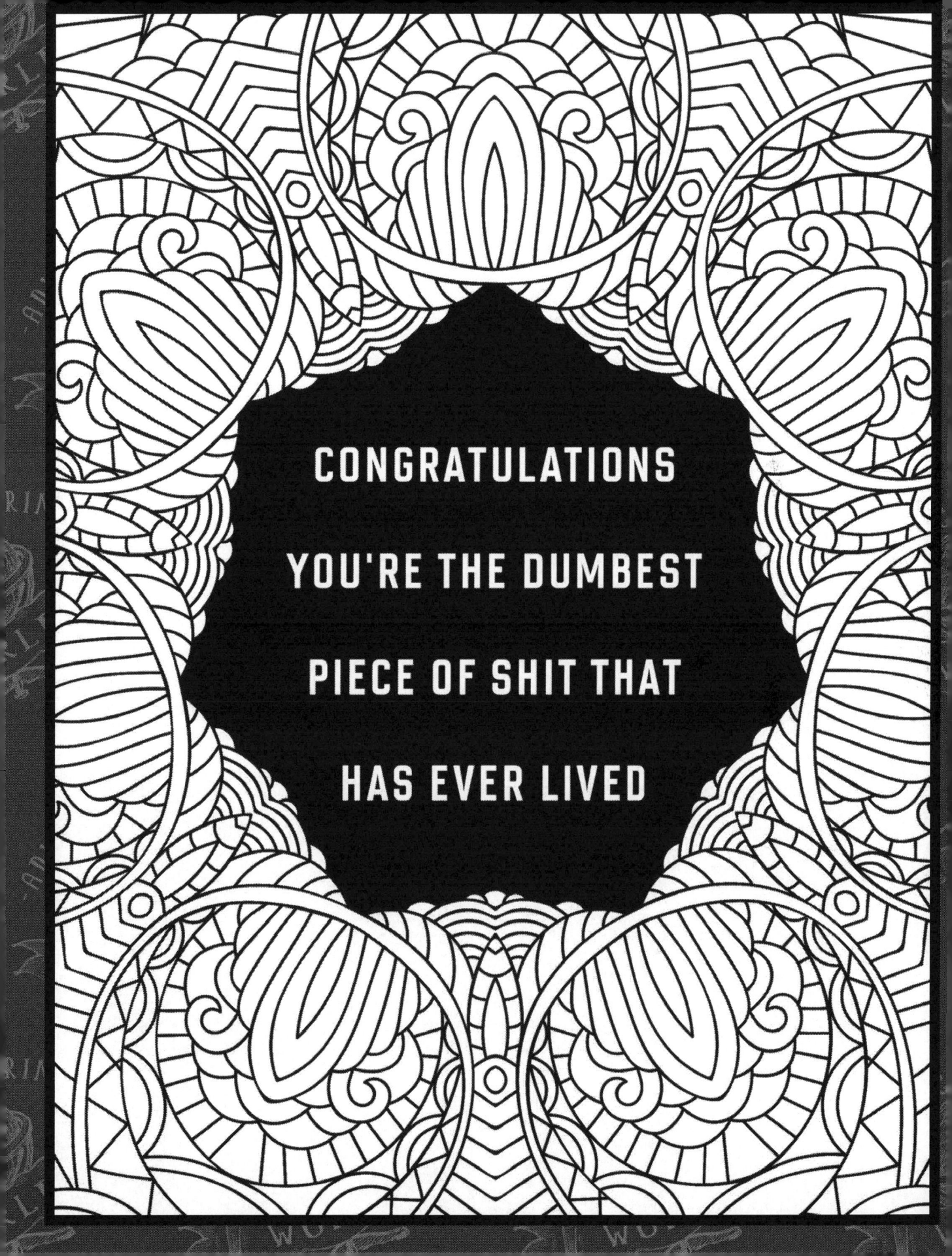

YOU'RE THE DUMBEST

PIECE OF SHIT THAT

HAS EVER LIVED

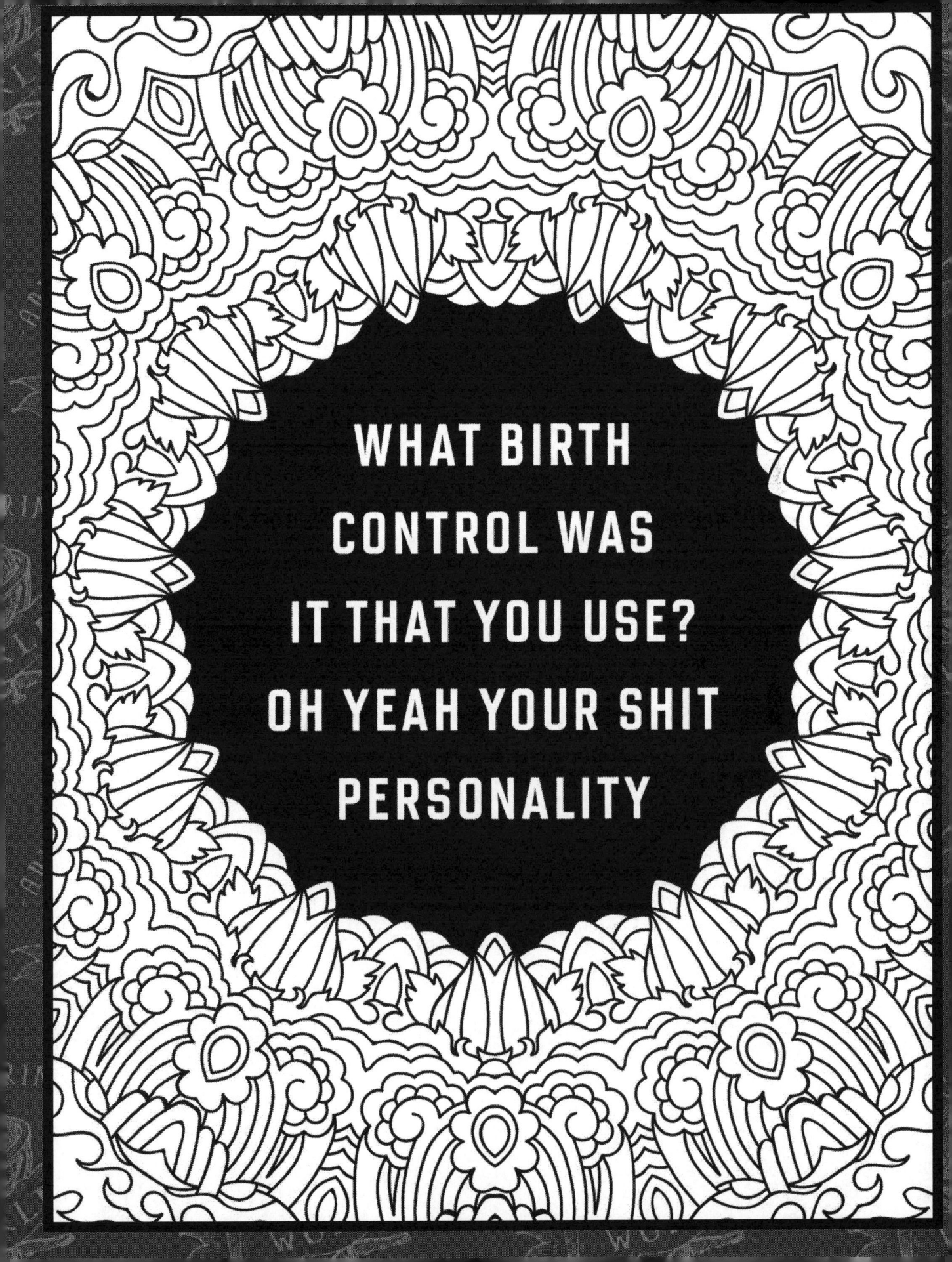

WHAT BIRTH CONTROL WAS IT THAT YOU USE? OH YEAH YOUR SHIT PERSONALITY

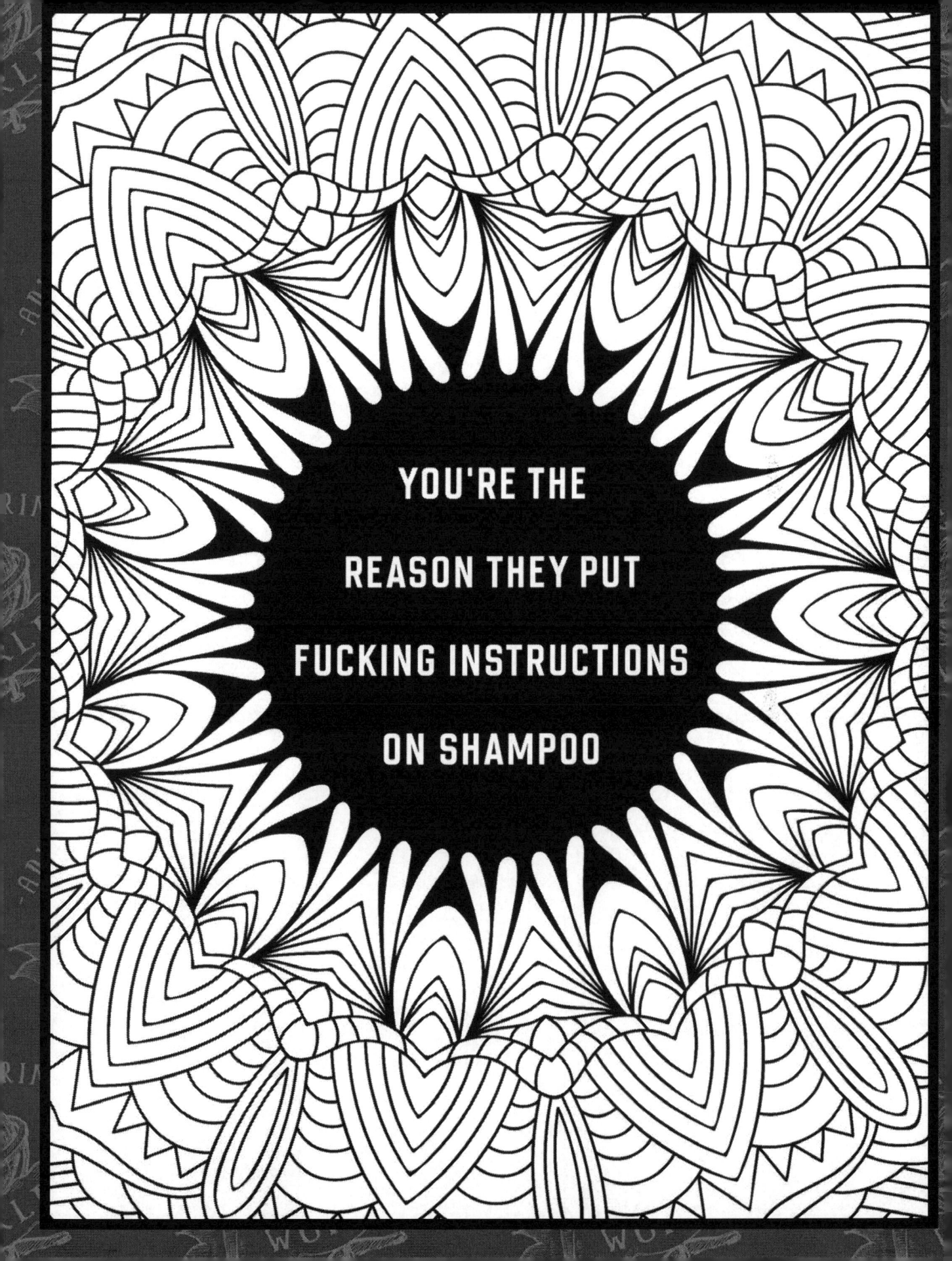

YOU'RE THE REASON THEY PUT FUCKING INSTRUCTIONS ON SHAMPOO

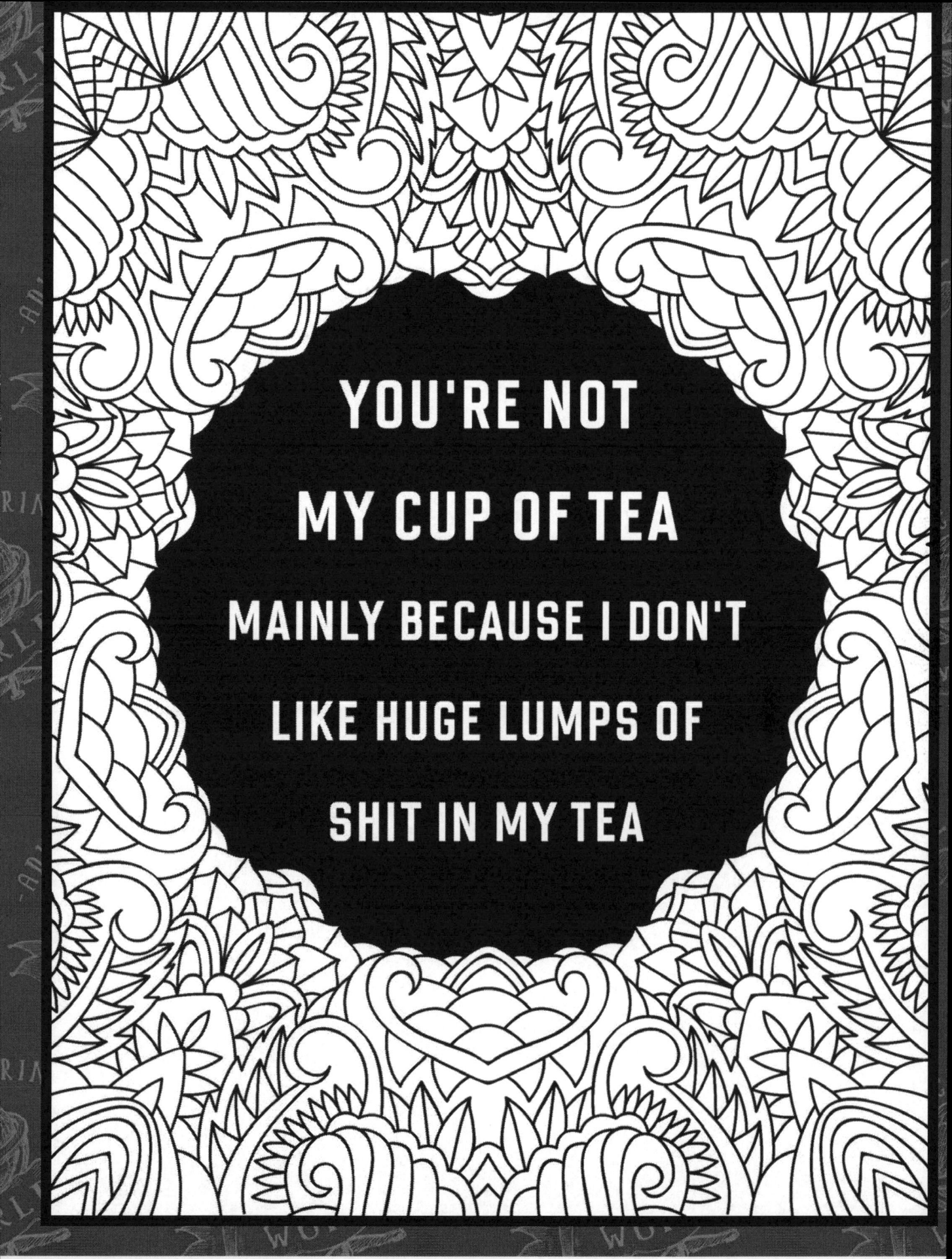

YOU'RE NOT MY CUP OF TEA MAINLY BECAUSE I DON'T LIKE HUGE LUMPS OF SHIT IN MY TEA

THERE IS NO

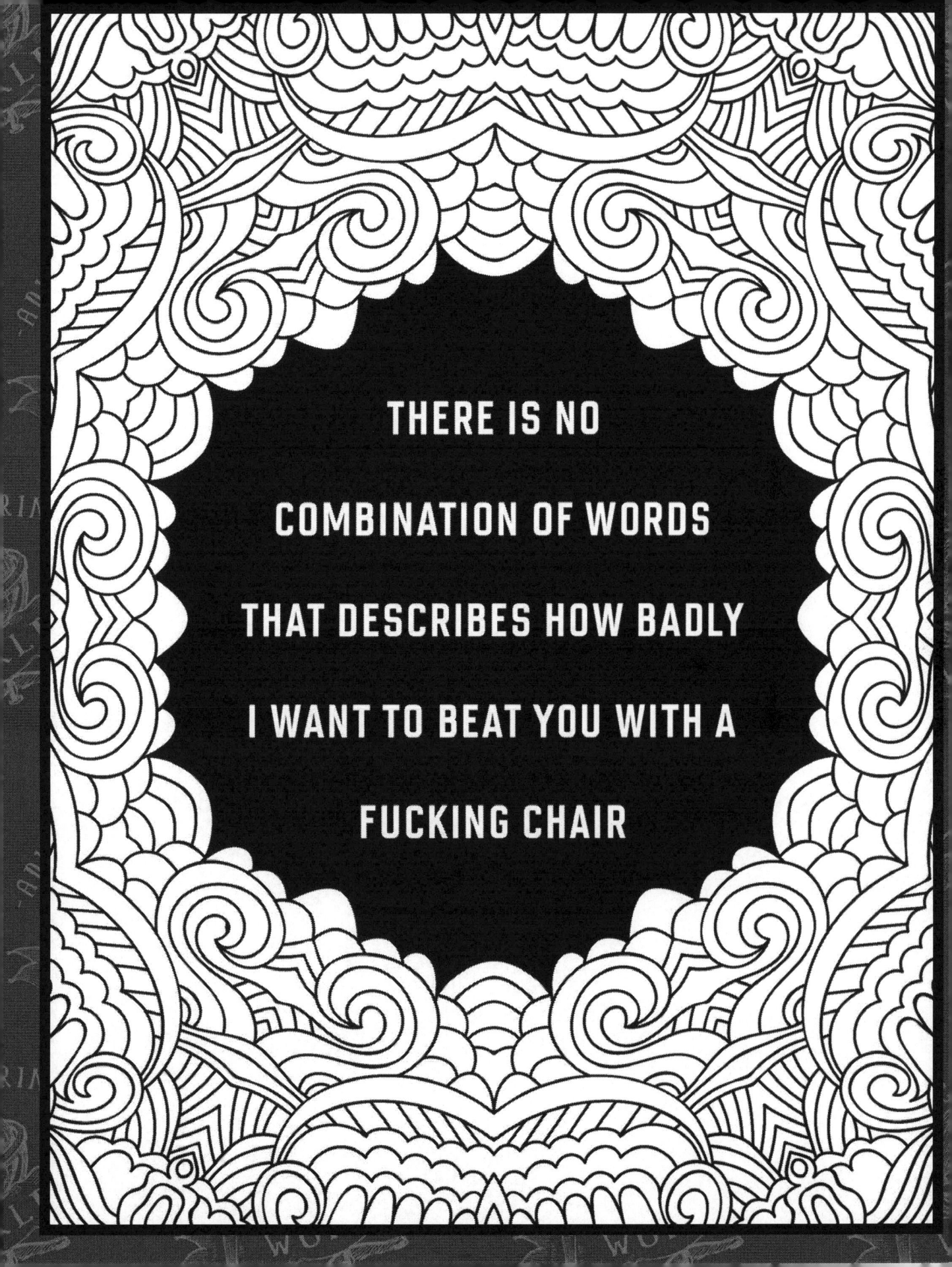

COMBINATION OF WORDS

THAT DESCRIBES HOW BADLY

I WANT TO BEAT YOU WITH A

FUCKING CHAIR

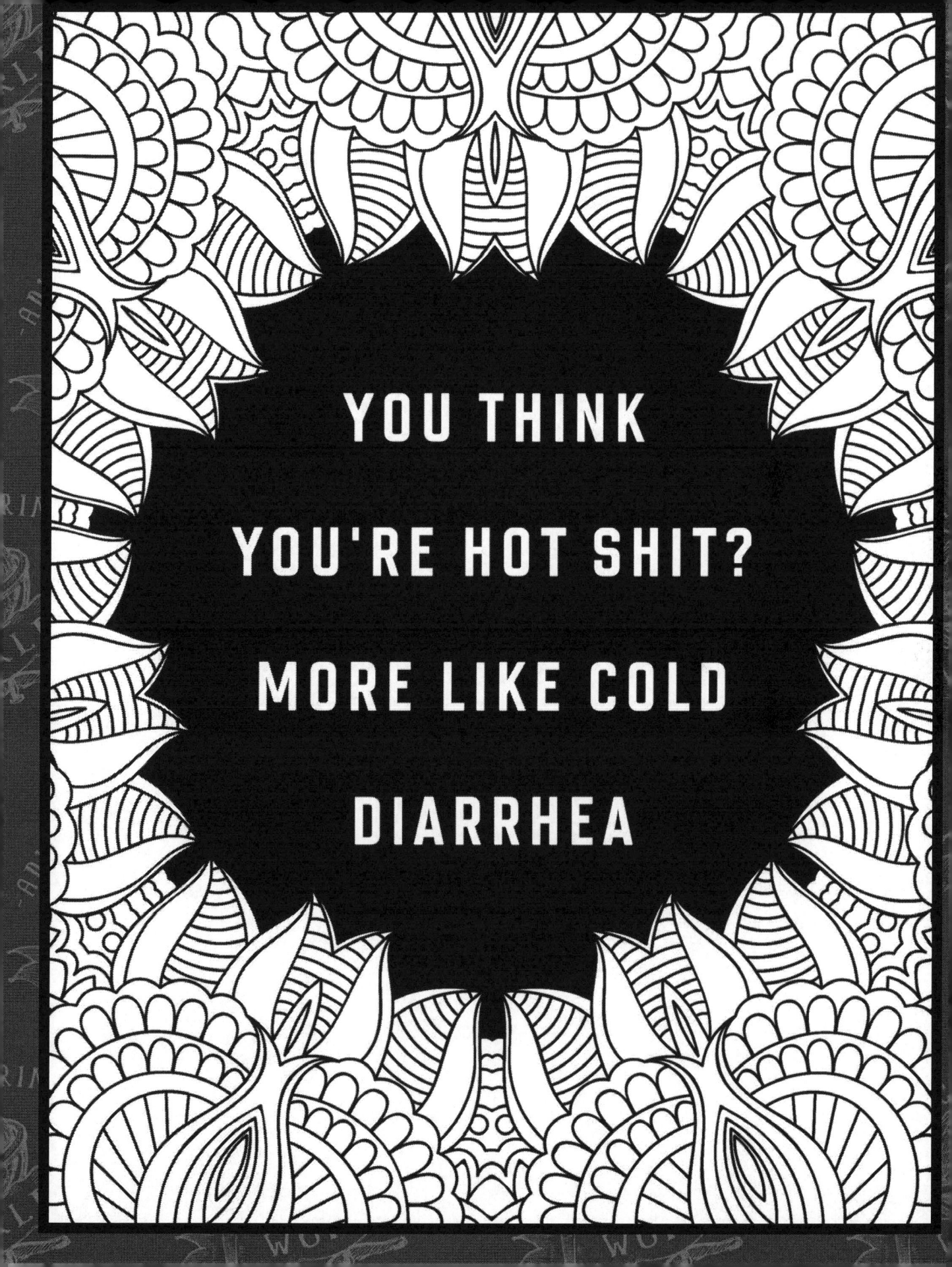

YOU THINK YOU'RE HOT SHIT? MORE LIKE COLD DIARRHEA

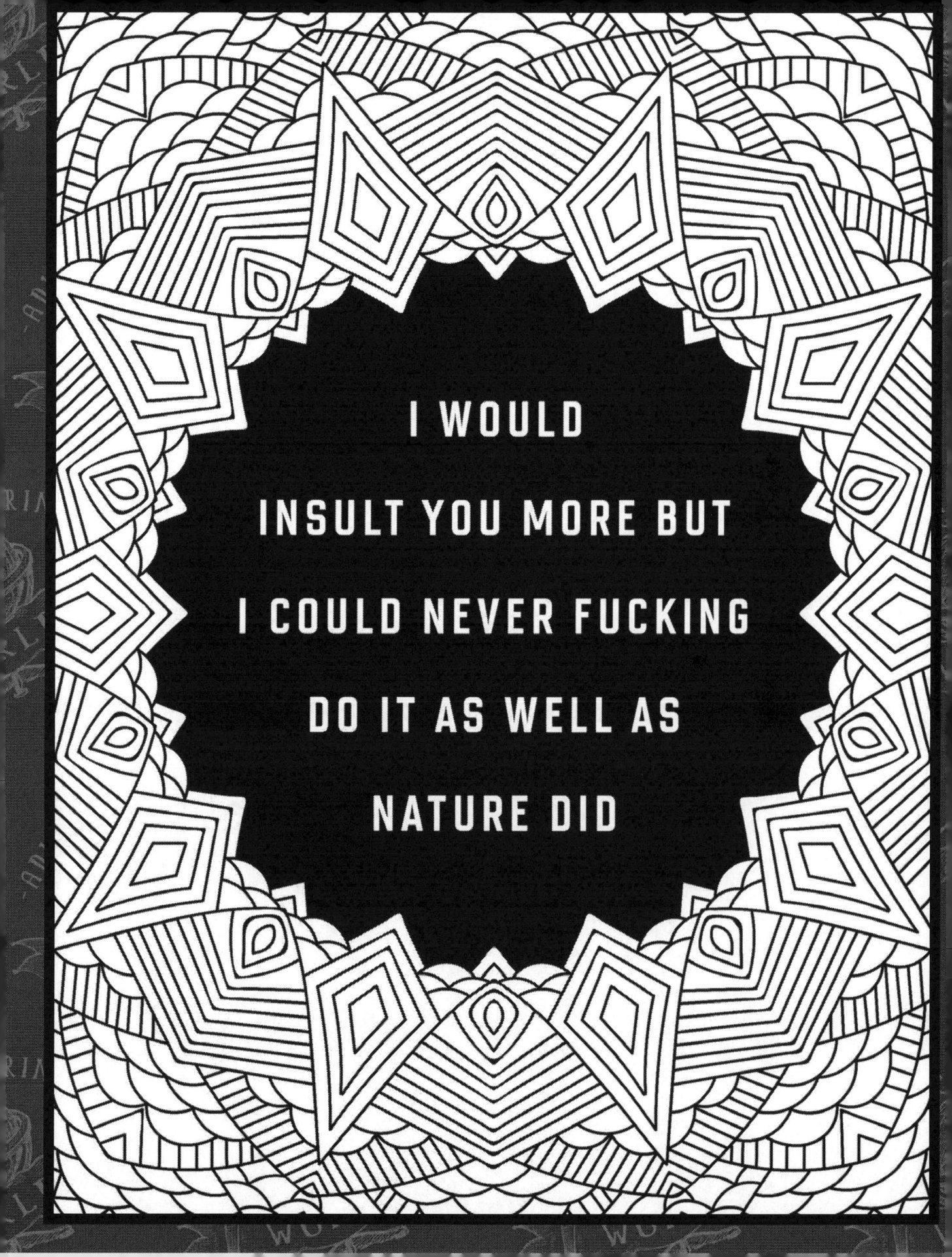

I WOULD INSULT YOU MORE BUT I COULD NEVER FUCKING DO IT AS WELL AS NATURE DID

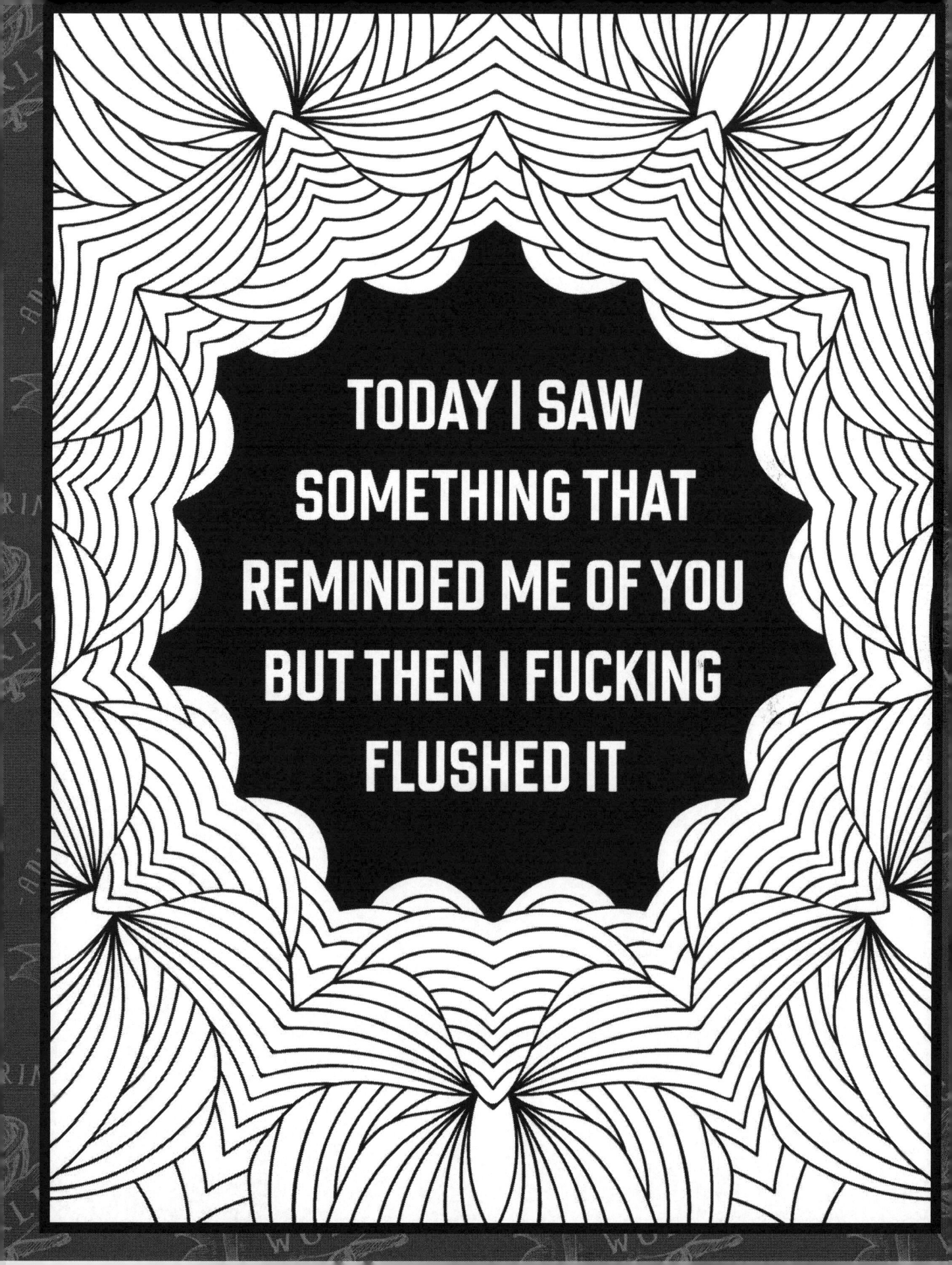

TODAY I SAW SOMETHING THAT REMINDED ME OF YOU BUT THEN I FUCKING FLUSHED IT

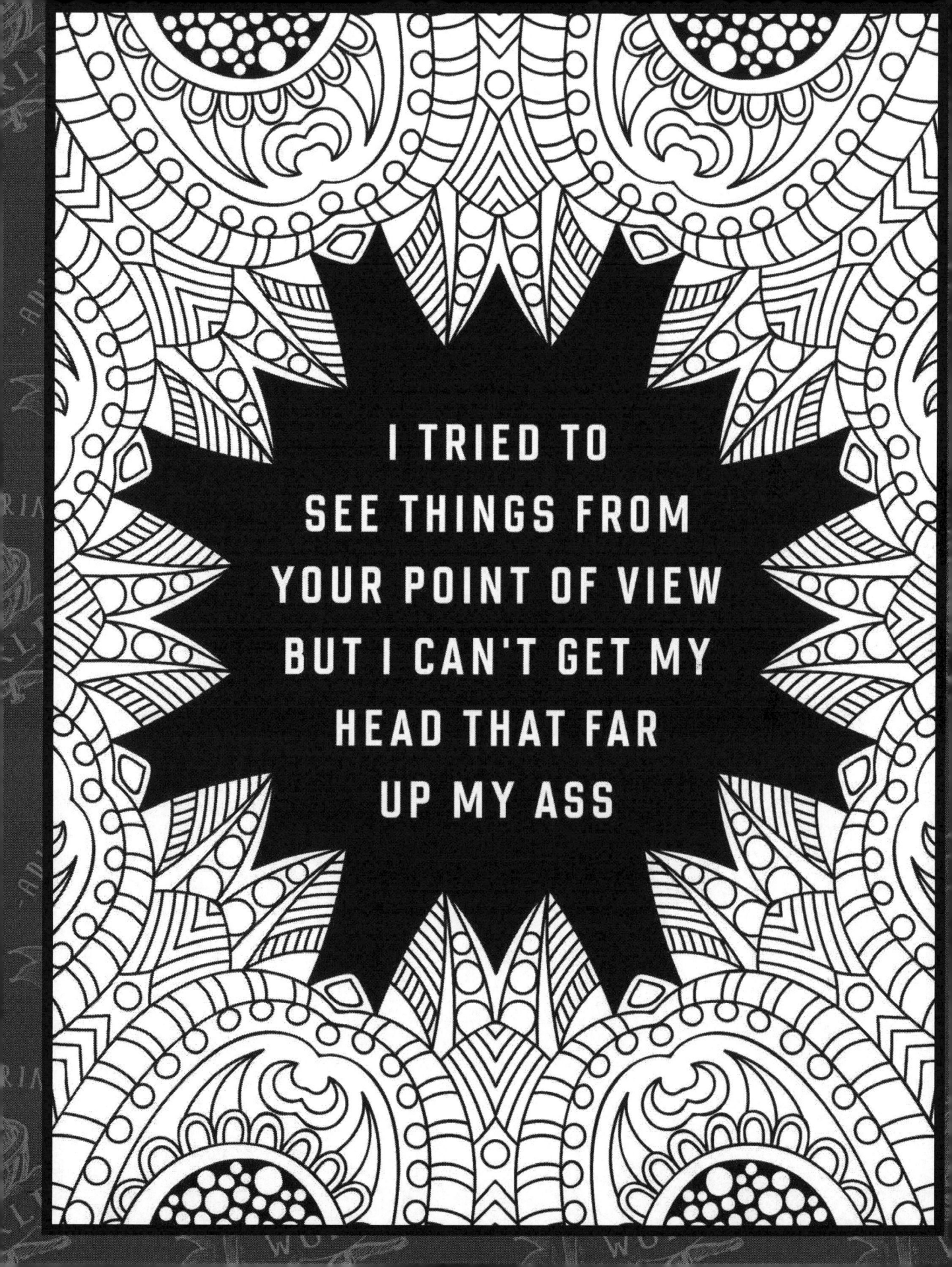

I TRIED TO SEE THINGS FROM YOUR POINT OF VIEW BUT I CAN'T GET MY HEAD THAT FAR UP MY ASS

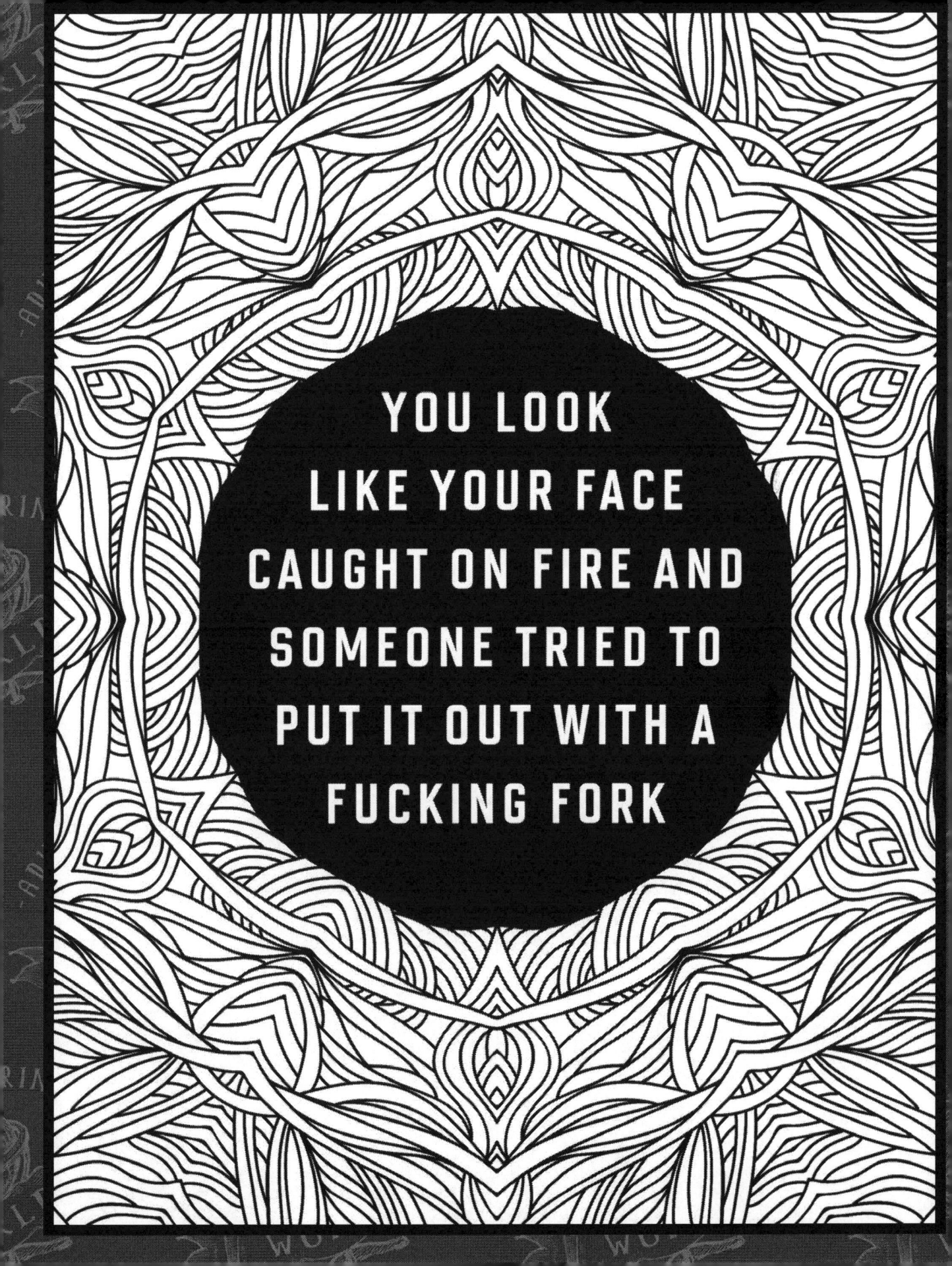

YOU LOOK LIKE YOUR FACE CAUGHT ON FIRE AND SOMEONE TRIED TO PUT IT OUT WITH A FUCKING FORK

I WOULDN'T EVEN PISS ON YOU IF YOU WERE ON FIRE

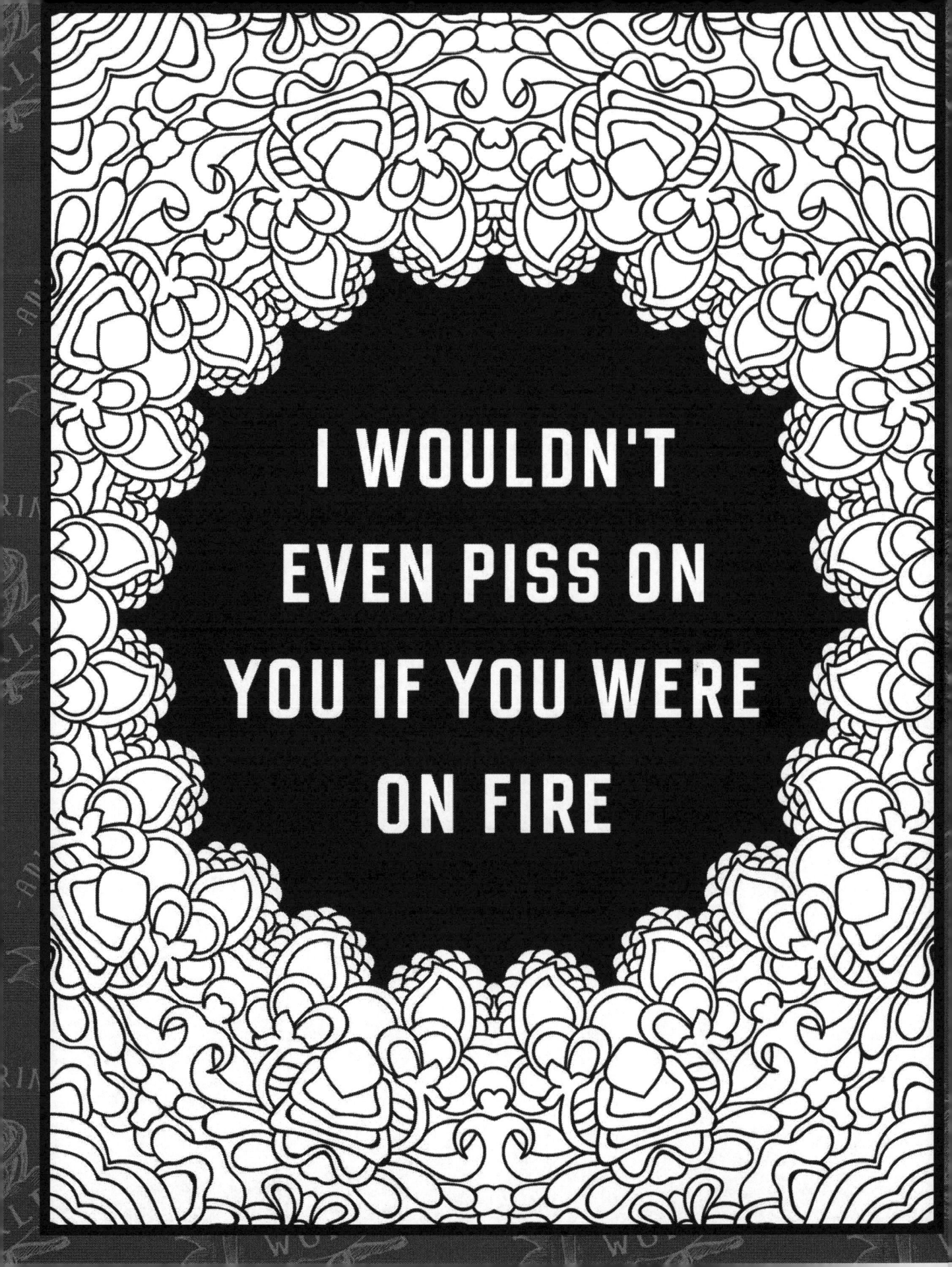

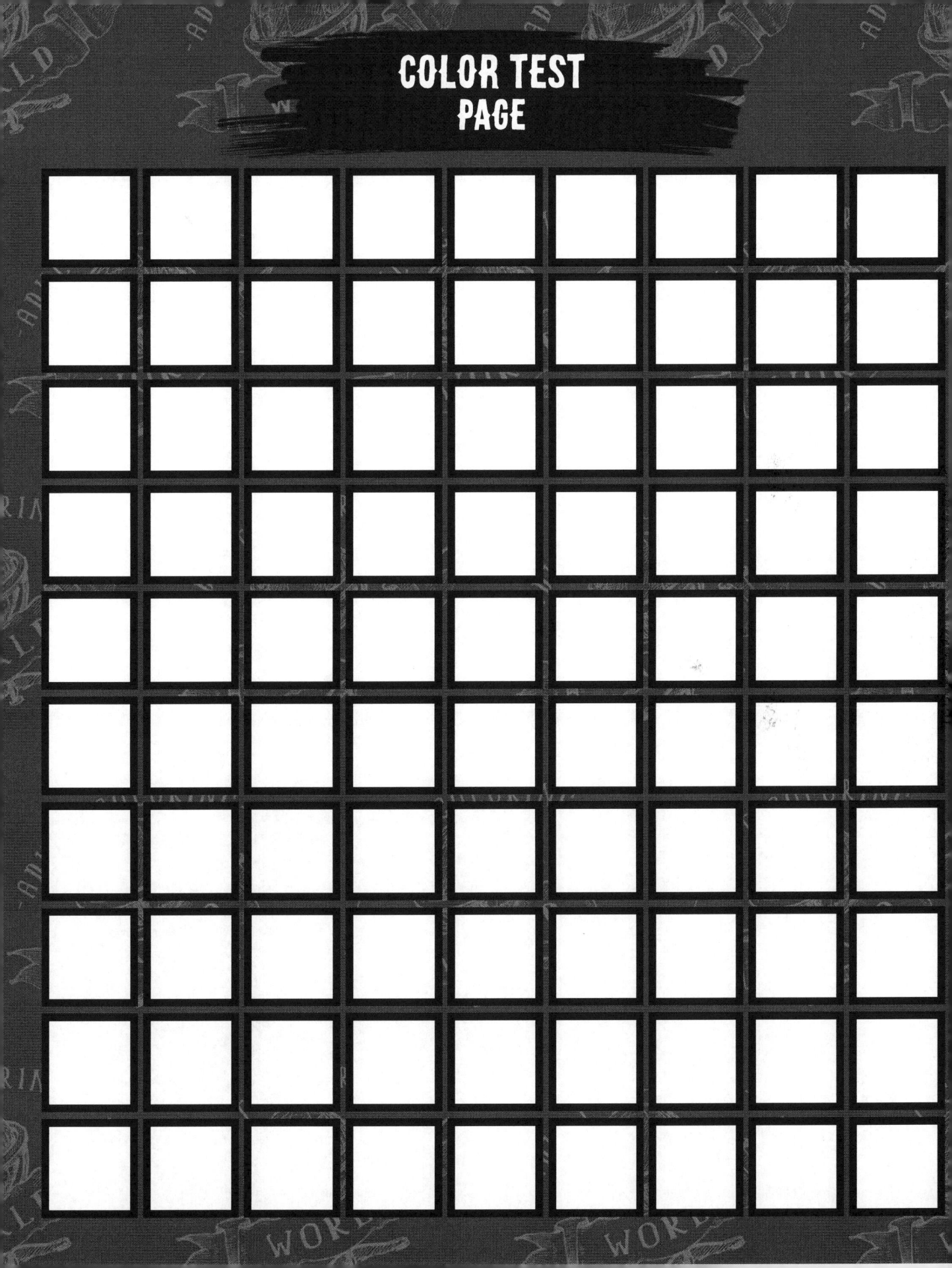

COLOR TEST PAGE

COLOR TEST PAGE

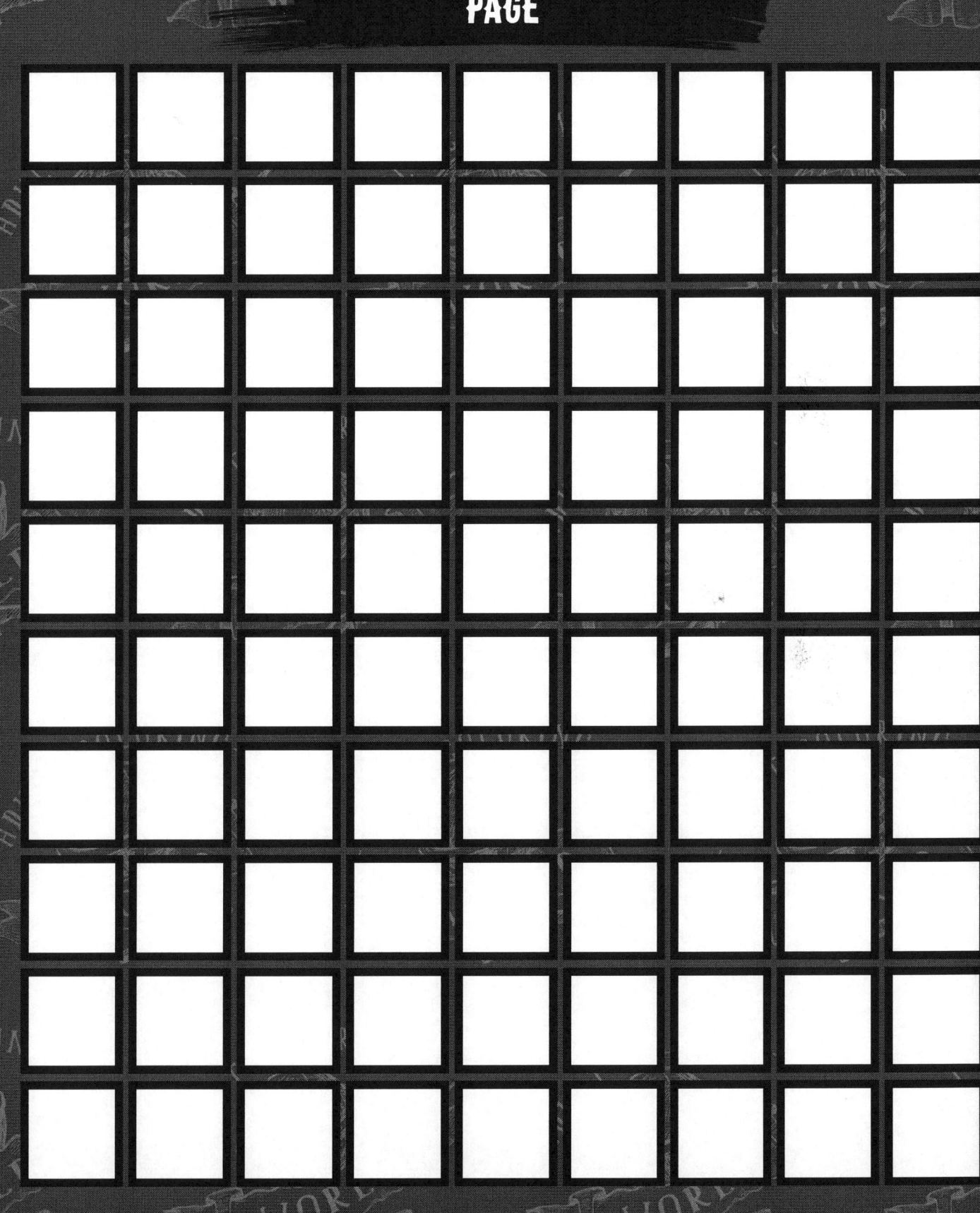

WE HOPE YOU ENJOYED THIS BOOK!

TO VIEW OUR HUGE RANGE OF ADULT COLORING BOOKS, VISIT OUR WEBSITE TODAY AND DON'T FORGET TO FOLLOW US VIA OUR SOCIAL ACCOUNTS!

ADULTCOLORINGWORLD.NET

- @adultcoloringworld
- facebook.com/adultcoloringworldbooks
- @adultcolorworld

Manufactured by Amazon.ca
Bolton, ON